May God increase your understanding as you experience a deeper walk through prayer.

TC Martin

Ask Seek Knock: There is An Answer

All rights reserved. No part of this book may be reproduced or transmitted in any form or by any means, electronic or mechanical, including photocopying, recording or any information storage and retrieval system without written permission of the publisher except for brief quotations used in reviews, written specifically for inclusion in a newspaper, blog, magazine, or academic paper.

Published by Krystal Lee Enterprises (KLE Publishing)
Copyright © 20201 by TC Martin All rights reserved.
Edited by K. Lee. Graphics by KLE.

Please send comments and questions:
Krystal Lee Enterprises
KLE Publishing Department

www.KLEPub.com   770-240-0089 Ext. 1
sales@klepub.com
Printed in the United States of America.

ISBN: 978-1-945066-05-4

Acknowledgments

First to God the Father and My Lord, savior Jesus Christ, I say thanks for Your reassurances, sustaining power, and trust that regardless of the facts in life, You provide. Father, You always know best what to do when I fall, no matter how many times. Having God in me, I am enthusiastic, full of resilience, and not yet finished.

My desire for everyone reading this book is to begin the process of having his or her relationship with God, through His Son Jesus Christ. Understanding prayer can set off a domino effect of success and high achievements in Him. For this reason, I humbly urge you to please consider joining me in cultivating this endeavor.

Words cannot express the level of gratitude I have for these individuals who have helped me grow as a person. In addition, those who have helped complete this book! I say thank you to my parents Domingo Octavio & Delores Martin for the opportunities I had—and still do, to dream because of the resources provided in sustaining my life. This would not have come to fruition without the stirring up of Apostle James & Prophetess Donna Duncan and H.E. The Right Honorable Dr. Phillips Phinn. "Thank you, for the guidance."

This idea was further pushed into reality because Bishop William Martin had a strong interest in seeing the dream of authoring my first book come to fruition. Next, this lady is a creative coach, author, editor, cheerleader, and mighty visionary, Dr. Krystal Lee (K. Lee). You put the time in to make ideas real, and your efforts in guiding the development of this manuscript are very much appreciated.

Kareem R. Vessup, Esquire, Carolyn S. Clyne, Esquire, Beverly Bejamin-George, Esquire, Dawnae Burwell & Darryl Warner thanks for all your assistance, endurance, and support in helping me finish a chapter well. Reverend Selwyn L. Davis, you are a man after God's heart! You will always be my Biblical professor. Bishop Darrell K. Dove Sr. and Morning Star Highway Church of Christ, thank you for all the genuine gratefulness expressed towards me.

Rev. Dr. Donald Odom your words and help are always welcomed, thank you! My big sisters, Dr. Alexis J.K. Williams, and the Institutional International Ministries, Brooklyn, NY. Min. Terrie Stevenson and Hope City Church in East New York, Prophetess Kelita Alston-Jones, RPA-C, Medical Director, and New Rivers of Life Church, Inc., Kenyetta Butler, and Leontyne Sanders thank you all for your advice.

Lavern Nelson nothing is ever complete without your input, you're a leading educator the world has yet to meet. Pastor Alida Williamson, the best is yet to come; I can see movies being made and us snacking on popcorn. Stay tune… Your love is genuine and thanks again for jumping in when needed. Words cannot express the gratitude I have for these individuals. I could not complete this without their necessary help. I am grateful to God for an awesome dream team that has confidence in me, even when I didn't believe it myself.

Lastly, I must say a big "Thank you" to Aoah Jackman, without you completing this book would have been difficult. And finally, to everyone who believed in this project, by taking their hard-earned money to pre-order, purchase, or join my mailing list to order when the book releases. I can now turn the page, complete this chapter, and on to my next book!

Love to these individuals and those I may have missed. Count it against my mind and not the heart.

TC Martin

Abstract

The King James Version of the Bible says this in Matthew 7:7-8:

7 Ask, and it shall be given you; seek, and ye shall find; knock, and it shall be opened unto you:

8 For every one that asketh receiveth; and he that seeketh findeth; and to him that knocketh it shall be opened.

The question many ask, is that I seek to find answers when they pray: to whom do they speak? When someone seeks, what exactly will they find through prayer? In knocking, what door are they knocking on, as far as, are there right and wrong ways to knock? Does a person have to be here or there? The scripture above leaves little to no room for someone or something who is asking, seeking, and knocking not to be found or presented with some answer they seek. It is my quest to find what is prayer. When somebody prays, to whom are they praying, deity, the atmosphere, or themselves? Why should someone pray? What is the purpose or benefit if any from prayer? Are there any important need-to-know items a person must be aware of for why a prayer(s) may not be answered? Lastly, is it possible to have unanswered prayers and if so, does prayer really work? It is my position and conclusion prayer still works today as it did in times of old. There is a way to pray, there are benefits to praying, and it is possible to have unanswered prayers, all the while prayers are still effective.

Table of Contents

Introduction/Executive Summary 9

What is Prayer 13

    Non Deity Prayers 14

    Deity Prayers 16

    Pagans and Magicians/Sorcerers 21

Who and to Whom 24

How to Pray 40

    Rituals, Traditions, Vs The Heart of Prayers .. 44

    Prayer Examples 53

    Body Language 60

When and Why Pray 70

    Watches 74

Prayer Still Works 83

Personal Testimony 102

Conclusion 105

Author 109

Bibliography 113

Introduction

There has been a lot of data generated on prayer to get estimates on who prays, how many people, and why. About 90 % of the US population or nine out of ten people pray and this rate has remained steady for over 50 years (Gallup and Lindsay 1999; Poloma and Gallup 1991). Of all the ethnic groups that pray, blacks, women, minority youth, and the elderly pray the most. The findings after concluding the trial lay claim to the fact prayer functions as a coping mechanism for people experiencing a strong emotion or life change (Sharp 2010:423).

Prayer cited by Bade and Cook are "thoughts, attitudes, and actions designed to express or experience connection to the sacred (McCullough and Larson 1999:86) and more simply as people's vehicle for communication with God (Matthews 1998:198):" (Bates and Cook 2008:123). According to the findings of Bates and Cook's study of Christian participants, they said prayer "calms me down, keeps me focused, gives me a ritual to fall back on, and decreases my fear (Bates and Cook

Introduction
2008:125)."

Rajeev Kurapati is an ICU medical professional working on the surgical floor. He does not claim to whom he prays, in that his religion is not announced in the article, but he says he prays for two reasons.

"1. No matter how much we advance as a species or what great technologies we invent, there will forever be situations that are just beyond our logic and rationale...[2] The word 'patient' means 'sufferer.' Patients expect doctors to alleviate all pain. I find the process of helping to get people out of their suffering the most satisfying experience of all (Kurapati 2013)."

Cohen, Wheeler, Scott, Edwards, Lusk, and the Anglican Working Group in Bioethics challenge the power of prayer but not its importance. They write in their article, Prayer as Therapy: A Challenge to Both Religious Belief and Professional Ethics:

"This [article] is not to declare that, according to theists, all studies of the import of prayer and religious belief for the health of patients are valueless. Nor is it to maintain that healthcare professionals must ignore the prayer practices and spiritual concerns of their patients. In a study conducted by the group, secretly praying for people in the coronary care unit, those prayed for had 10 percent fewer complications than those who had no one assigned to pray for them (2000:40)."

Prayer differs from asking to wishing, from hoping to communication, and then to performing rites. Although the reason people pray or perform ceremonies differs from worship to tradition, and gaining control over a deity's proposed power or oneself, prayer appears to work. Prayer as it were 30 or 40 years ago on a percentage scale maintains the ratio for each ethnic group that prays or believes in God. Blacks pray the most, followed by the elderly and women, and the white male prays the least (Baker 2008:178).

Pew Research finds that Black Millennials are more religious than other millennials. Diamant and Mohamed found in their study that reported on the Pew Research website:

"…nearly two-thirds (64%) of black Millennials are highly religious on a four-item scale of religious commitment – which includes belief in God and self-described importance of religion, in addition to prayer and worship attendance – compared with 39% of non-black Millennials (Diamant and Mohamed 2018)."

In another Pew Research published article by David Masci, he discovers that 79% of Blacks in America identify as Christian and 83% of them believe in the existence of God compared to 70% of Whites and 77% of Hispanics that are Christian. 61% of Whites say there is a God and 59% of Hispanics say the same.

Identifying as Christian doesn't mean any other ways of life or reasons for being are not being considered. In this writing, I expect to cross-examine research, trains of thought, and results provided by numerous authors using various techniques to arrive at their concluded thoughts. I furthermore anticipate, discussing and proving how even the atheist that professes there is no God, when times get difficult, they too may find comfort in running to a cross, idol, or religion even if

Introduction

briefly to cope with unexplainable events or health concerns. Prayer has been a leading force that helped shape cultures, governments, ideologies, clothing, ways of life, and expectations for what is holy, good, or heathen.

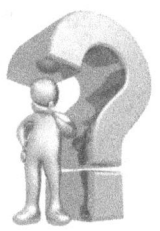

"What"

Speaking with Judeo-Christians, many conclude prayer is equivalent to communicating with God. Prayer is something reserved for the greatest and most powerful being that has ever been or will be. The Alpha and Omega, have no beginning and no end. This conclusion is not accepted by all, and some feel that prayer is simply talking to anyone or anything that would have an ear to hear. Or perhaps, a being that simple can be in tune with a person's inner thoughts, and observe their actions; that being could be a deeper committed version of oneself (Gross 2002:84). This is also disagreeable by those who determine prayer is a summoning, a means to control a deity's power and influence on earth.

I have studied three different approaches that differences in opinion must be discussed. The non-deity prayers, the deity prayers, or those that pray to many gods and sorcerers/magicians. The non-deity prayers, would not use the word pray to mean much more than wishing, hoping, hence praying, unlike monotheistic prayers. Groups belonging to this ideology include

What rationalists, atheists, agnostics, and Buddhists to name a few. Many persons reflected in this group, may use the word "pray," but it is used as more of a figure of speech than what is intended by Bible-believing Christians.

Non-Deity Prayers

Buddhists for example, do not identify that there is any deity controlling or sovereign on the earth. Simply put, "Buddhism is one of the world's few nontheistic religions, denying the existence (or, more accurately, the relevance) of any transcendent, external supreme being who created the world and bestows salvation on followers of that religion."

This opinion is in stark separation from what Christians believe—this concept is at the bedrock of a Christian's faith. Furthermore, salvation is the only promise given to man that would make them want to spend their life serving God and not themselves. Christians give up their life, in that they allow God's thought to be their thoughts, so that they may find themselves. A scripture that coins this understanding is: "For whosoever will save his life shall lose it: and whosoever will lose his life for my sake shall find it. (Matthew 16:25 KJV)."

Interestingly put, Rita M. Gross, states in her article Meditation and Prayer: A Comparative Inquiry, that Christians pray and Buddhists meditate, but she thinks the difference between praying and meditation is not that big of a deal. Her prayers may have the same words as a Christian, minus the God reference, and she believes this detail is minor. This seems untrue when thinking of what is a prayer to Christians.

So, to the contrary, leaving God out of prayer is like trying to send a piece of mail to someone with no address in the " to" column; and if there were an addressee, it would be to a deeper consciousness perhaps of oneself. Within this same article she writes that Buddhist pray, but these words are addressed to a visualized being whose symbolic form represents ultimate reality and one's true being (Gross 2002:84). Although Buddhists recognize Buddha, they don't do so in the same way as Christians acknowledge God; some Buddhist may even believe in superhumans and their ability to impact the future, but they don't see these creatures as solid beings.

The Buddhists it would appear see them as beings that only exist because they exist, and they are in tune with their deeper and enlightened self and that has manifested these beings to be seen. To further explain, angels and spirits do not exist if God does not exist. These creatures only exist like how Christians believe God exists. Their existence seems to be predicated on the person's belief.

Meditating is what the author claimed a Buddhist does, but what exactly does that mean? How does meditating differ from what a Buddhist does compared to a Christian? Meditation on the onset, would appear to be a synonym for prayer. To define meditation according to a Buddhist, it is a sequence of words spoken or unspoken not directed to any specific solid being, but ideally intended for the deeper self and not the ego (Gross 2002:84).

Meditating consists of three types of prayers for

What
the Buddhist according to the article: 1: prayers to many relatively existing beings. 2: aspirations or wishes, the third, most elusive type of Buddhist utterance comes from the liturgies of Tibetan "deity yoga." These prayers are non-dualistic, non-theistic theological context could seem like a theological absurdity (Gross 2002:79).

Some Buddhists see meditation and prayer as wishing, but they expect nothing to come from it. In fact, to pray as a true Buddhist, a person must expect nothing from their prayers. Half of them believe there is no one out there, no enlightened being beyond themselves, that can impact their life. The other believes they are doing nothing more than wishing and saying it into the air without expectation.

Another group that believes there is no deity to catch the prayers of man, is a rationalist. Many of them ration that there is no God and if it is, He does not hear or respond to man's prayers because that would not be fair. How can anyone communicate with the True and divine God and not shake up the world? Furthermore, how can anyone suffer, die, or experience misfortune if there were a God? So they conclude, that prayer means nothing.

Starting this dialogue on meditation a contrast has to be presented as to how these types of prayers are different from the concept of a praying Christian, then perhaps, how prayer is different amongst Protestants and Catholics.

Deity Prayers

Deity prayers are people of faiths and religions that believe there is a supreme being and that being cares for man. This being is high and lifted up, but through prayer, God can be reached. Prayer is a line of open communication of contact between a person and someone divine.

Eliezer Finkelman defines the concept of prayer to mean expressing one's yearning to God, and if God was not in the picture, it would denote making a wish (Finkelman 2016-2017:125). Christians believe and understand that prayer ought to be a part of their everyday life. Prayer is viewed as communicating, speaking with, or requesting something from God. Jurgen Moltmann wrote in the article "What Are We Doing When We Pray?" that prayers are:

"…ways of expressing our lives before God. To call them all praying is much too narrow, because the word pray means much the same as ask and plead. But to come to God only with our entreaties is hardly the expression of a true love for God. God is more than our heavenly helper in time of need (Moltmann 1997:92)."

Unlike meditation, when a Christian prays they are told to believe they have what they ask for and that God hears their prayers. Prayers in a sense, are a means of traveling from earth into the presence of God. It is a much deeper experience for some who pray juxtaposed to others who are praying.

The Bible does not clearly define what prayer is, as far as give a defined definition. Prayer is spoken about in the ways in which it should be done, why, and how. To ascertain what prayer is, one must first define what types of prayers are made to God by Christians.

What

The most pivotal prayer of all prayers could arguably be the sinners' prayer. It is believed that this prayer must predate any other prayer because this prayer grants access if it will be granted to the one praying. John 9:31 reads: "Now we know that God heareth not sinners: but if any man be a worshipper of God, and doeth his will, him he heareth."

A second prayer type includes a request being made to God. Unlike a wish that is spoken out into the atmosphere, that doesn't rely on any outside force directly to interfere in a situation, prayer begs for God's involvement. It is a request one makes to God to intercede in what may mean something very great or simple to the person.

A third kind of prayer is asking. Many questions are asked by either one person to another, or to oneself. Unlike non-deity persons who pray, Christians focus on the response they receive from God through prayer and some may argue on one's reality. If a person prays, they must also be prepared to listen. So, prayer is asking and listening, furthermore, to listen one must spend time and wait.

The fourth prayer is giving thanks. Christians don't simply use prayer as a means of getting things from God, but also to acknowledge and thank Him for what He has already done. And the fifth is similar, to give God worship. Although there are many types of prayers, one form of prayer that God requests not to be offered to him is chanting.

Prayer is not repeating the same thing over and over again, or zoning out, meditating, in a sense that the person continues to pray the same line repeatedly. Matthew 6:7 says, "But when ye pray, use not vain repetitions, as the heathen do: for they think that they shall be heard for their much speaking."

To continue the contrast of what is different between a Buddhist meditating and a Christian, one has to ask a simple question. What is the focus of that meditation, or prayer? Meditation as defined from a Christian perspective can be related to prayer, if the purpose for meditation is defined as the Bible commands. In Joshua 1:8 it reads: "This book of the law shall not depart out of thy mouth, but thou shalt meditate therein day and night, that thou mayest observe to do according to all that is written therein: for then thou shalt make thy way prosperous, and then thou shalt have good success."

Meditating according to this instruction, doesn't simply mean repeating the Word day and night, like perhaps a Buddhist monk, but thinking about the Word day and night. Speak what is written so that a person's thoughts conform to the ways and truths of the Divine. Pray the Word to God, and Christians believe that as they seek, through prayer, they will find. As they knock, bringing the petition, questions, or problems to God He will answer.

Two other unique monotheistic prayers that should be included in the conversation of what is prayer as it pertains to praying to a deity are Muslims and Jews. These two religions are opposites when it pertains to everything social perhaps, but they are similar in the way they define prayer.

The Muslim defines prayer as a means for Allah,

What known to others perhaps as God, to speak to his/His subjects. The conversational aspects that the Christian enjoys, are not the same for the Muslim or Jew. Prayers among these people groups are designed to hear from God. Knohl says this in Between Voice and Silence: The Relationship Between Prayer and Temple Cult:

"Moreover, in the work of this school, there is no connection of direct speech between God and Israel; only Moses himself hears God's word. Indeed, even the verbal connection with Moses is one-sided: God turns to Moses and speaks to him, but there is no speech of Moses to God (Knohl 1996:20)!"

The concept of a back-and-forth connection, or two-way line of communication that the Christian believes arguably about the same God as the Jew, appears to have two very different understandings of what prayer is or how it is defined. Knohl argues that petitional prayer and hymns of thanksgiving, offered by Christians in prayer and perhaps the melodic tone of a Muslim prayer call are permeated with anthropomorphic language concerning God. He further points to how priestly teaching tends to reject anthropomorphic and anthropopathic imagery (Knohl 1996:20).

Knohl's writing spoke excessively of separating divine prayer from pagan prayers. The Muslim too takes great aim so as to not water down the process and importance of prayer to that of pagans. Those that are pagan, tend to offer words and other performances, as a form of prayer and worship to address as many gods as they hope would listen or grant them audience.

Pagans and Magicians/Sorcerers

The pagan doesn't believe in one source, one supreme being per se, but in multiple gods that may all have equally or slightly variant powers. "[The pagan further] believes in a world governed by numerous forces, some unconscious but many conscious. He addresses his prayers to one of the forces, thinking that it might pay attention to his needs and that it, though in conflict with other powers, might have enough power to help him (Finkelman 2016-2017:126)." A Christian, Jew, or Muslim who prays believes their prayers are going to the only true God of their faith and is in no race to reach one of many gods to receive help.

A pagan, for that matter, uses prayer to address a being to help them and grant their wishes/petitions, but they don't have one solitary being they pray to but many for a similar effect. The pagan also doesn't look at prayer as a form of communication, but much like magic. The theurgist, perhaps closely identified to being a kind of magician, may also be thrown in the pot with a pagan, but the magician is not one who prays but performs rites (Finkelman 2016-2017:126).

People who agree with the thought of Israel Knohl, Eliezer Finkelman, and Liz James who see prayer as magic, see prayer as a means to reach out to a conscious or unconscious entity to try and control that beings' power. Prayer in this sense is not prayer, because a request is not being made, as much as a demand is going forth based on a ritual they perform to grant access to powers that may or may not be.

The Bible clearly speaks about Christians not comingling with those who try to use dark arts to

What progress or get their wishes granted. Many people that belong to this category, or form of praying if that word could even loosely be used, do so to channel spirits through psychics, witches, and warlocks tactics. Although chanting is involved with such processes, it is not compared to prayer, because prayer tends to be associated with God and those that see whatever god or essence they pray to, to be good, and have good intentions towards people.

On the contrary, those who use manipulation in their prayers are not seeking the good in whatever they find, but already tapped into the darkness that lies within them. To perform magic, rituals, or rites, one often is not seeking the goodness in a supreme being but something more sinister.

Although these very different groups pray, their ideals for what prayer is change the why, how, and when they pray. Depending on if the prayer is a Buddhist, Christian, Muslim, Jew, pagan, witch, psychic, or warlock, prayer can be something as meaningful as transitioning in between worlds, seeing the world through The Creator of the Universe's eyes, or as grim as channeling demonic spirits to get a desired outcome.

TC Martin

Who and To Whom

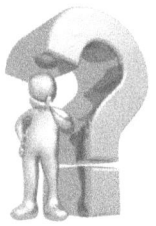

"Who and to Whom"

A very simple question with a not-so-forward answer, who is a person talking to when they pray? Like anything in life, when considering the person a message is intended for, language, empathy, and inflection varies. If a person is talking to a child, they may use baby language, soft words, and may appear to be very understanding. If that same person is getting married, they may be more forceful about what they want and don't want.

Likewise, if they are a CEO communicating with staff, they may talk differently than if they were at church or among friends. Certain characters do impact a person's speech. Although man would like to think they are always the same no matter the occasion, the truth, is there an alternative version of ourselves—that depends on the situation and the audience if it appears.

Changing communication styles doesn't make a person phony, not being genuine, or sincere, however, changes everything. A popular analogy for this character flaw is two-faced, but that is not what Christians believe they do when they change into the best selves they can muster to address God. The audience for when Christians pray is God; God as in the Creator of the Universe, The Great I Am, and Abba Father.

Before anyone talks to someone to appeal, there would be questions that must be answered. A salesperson does not seek to get a sale by knowing nothing about their potential clients. A man doesn't offer to marry a woman without knowing something about her character, family background, history, medical status, etc. These are need-to-know things so that if you want kids, and she can't have them, he would have a decision to make.

The Bible says, "Taste me to know that I am good (Psalm 34:8)." This simply put means to get to know God's character and understand what He requires. Yes, the Bible says for people to lay aside every weight that will hinder them, sin (Hebrews 12:1), but in separating oneself from sin, the person will be changed by His presence. Although there are mentions of scriptures that compare God the Creator, as a father to the fatherless, mother to the motherless, hope to the hopeless, etc. (Genesis 1:1, Psalm 68:5, Isaiah 41:10); the Bible is clear God the Father is not a man (Numbers 23:19) but the spirit (John 4:24).

Unlike what Eliezer Finkelman writes, "When we express our prayers, our requests, to that benevolent personage, I mean, God, philosophers, and other believers address a person-like entity (Finkelman 2016-2017:127)." If this is the case, an argument for idolatry may be presented. If we think of a specific image, man or woman, to represent God, like the Zeus character

Who and To Whom

drawn and depicted in ancient buildings, Christians do not understand to whom they are praying. The Bible says not to worship any images, or give special privileges to relics, statues, or icons because that would end like in the case of Rachel with Israel and the Hebrews with the Golden Calf.

Unlike pagans, who pray to images carved in stone, or wood, who don't move or make anything happen as a requirement for their belief, it is a punishment for Christians to pray and put their hope in an idol. Deuteronomy 4:28 says, "And there ye shall serve gods, the work of men's hands, wood, and stone, which neither see, nor hear, nor eat, nor smell." God is a living, breathing, seeing, hearing, smelling, and working deity (2 Corinthians 2:15, Leviticus 1:1-17, Genesis 2:7, Philippians 1:6). In the following verse of Deuteronomy 4:29 it reads, "But if from thence thou shalt seek the Lord thy God, thou shalt find him if thou seek him with all thy heart and with all thy soul." He has the power to make the impossible, possible (Luke 18:27). Things that are impossible for man, are possible with God the Bible says.

Some might argue, but what about people who pray, and the God of the Christians is not the intended listener, who are they praying to or summoning? Do these prayers mean anything, and if they don't, why does it seem like some of them get what they ask and others do not? Because many of the studies presented in this research are from a Christian perspective, as much of the Western world is Christian (Masci 2018), turning to the Bible admits that there are spirits that war against man. This war is against fallen angels, demons, principalities of darkness, powers, the devil, and spiritual wickedness in high places (Ephesians 6:12).

Some perform rites and the audience they seek is not of God the Creator, but to sinister spirits, lesser gods, the prince of the air (Satan). Some may not realize they are praying to idols, because their faith permits them praying to statues as a means of respect to Christian influences. For example, it is not uncommon for Catholics to pray to the Mother Mary statue. For some Christians, it is normal to look at a white male with a crown of thorns nailed to a cross and feel compelled to pray even to look upon the statue as they perform such prayers. Within the findings of Liz James, she writes about statue worship and icons and discusses differences if any between Christian images, idols, statues, and those of pagans. She writes:

"Consequently, it is unsurprising that so much effort was spent in the period of Iconoclasm in trying to establish a difference between "idols" and "images." … As such, it reflects the dispute about icons and their miraculous powers with stories about the powers of pagan images. Both Iconophile folklore and Iconoclast polemic share the same subtext as the Parastaseis: the image and its miraculous power. Kazhdan suggests that the Parastaseis can be interpreted as an Iconophile text, written by those who favored icons in a bid to counteract Iconoclast propaganda. By telling stories about pagan statues that only brought injury and death, these images could be contrasted unfavorably with Christian icons which worked only beneficial miracles. But, as I have shown above, Christian images were as ready as pagan ones to strike down those who tampered with them (James 1996:16)."

Who and To Whom

How is it that Christians have images at all if one of the 10 commandments was to not have any graven images, that also includes idols, they worship, hence pray to (Exodus 20:4); because their God is in heaven. He is not locked away in an image, idol, or statue, but He lives unlike the pagan statues! Many times God tells different authors to write about the contrast between Christians to pagans, there should be no ground to unify the two groups, as one believes in many gods (little "g") and the Christians believe in the only God. So why are or were, both groups so set on defending statues that could not defend themselves?

If Leviticus 20:4 wasn't clear, the following is stated in Leviticus 26:1, "Ye shall make you no idols nor grave image, neither rear you up a standing image, neither shall ye set up any image of stone in your land, to bow down unto it: for I am the Lord your God." Christians are forbidden, like Muslims and Jews, to address their prayers to anything, person, or deity that is not God. In other words:

"In Abrahamic religions, namely Christianity, Islam, and Judaism, idolatry connotes the worship of something or someone other than God as if it were God. In these monotheistic religions, idolatry has been considered the "worship of false gods" and is forbidden by values such as the Ten Commandments (Wikipedia 2019)."

Another crucial debate amongst Christians is, "Do or are Christians supposed to pray to Jesus?" The Catholic Layman writes, "He is commonly pictured either as an infant in his mother's arms, or as in the agonies of death on the cross; neither of these representations bring him before the mind as one ready to hear and answer the requests of his people, those who have not some other means of studying his character are in danger of losing sight of some of the most important practical lessons taught us by our Savior's incarnation (The Catholic Layman 1852:64)." The question, is this what the Bible meant when the instruction was given to pray in Jesus name (John 14:13-14)?

Scriptures point to Jesus being the Word made into flesh (John 1:14), so to pray in Jesus' name, may imply praying the Word, not to the man. An issue that Jewish priests raise against praying to a personified being of God, is that it runs the line of being pagan, magic, and not in right standing. Knohl wrote, "Prayer to a personal God, by contrast, which is removed from magic but contains some elements of personification of God, is inconsistent with Priestly theology and, for this reason, has no place in the Temple (Knohl 1996:20-21)." Like a Christian, to pray to a man, or personified being, even if it is Jesus, is inconsistent with a monotheistic faith which believes in one divine authority.

So, who is this God that requires no other thing to supersede His influence, power, and majesty among His chosen? This God is "holy (1 Samuel 2:2, Isaiah 6:3)," "omnipotent," "sovereign," "all-powerful (Ephesians 1:19)," the creator of life and every good thing (Nehemiah 9:6, James 1:17)." He is God over all but not God to all. Everyone who calls Him Lord does not do so out of worship, but for some only because that is His name. Christians believe they must have a relationship with God, in order to be a chosen one of His.

John Calvin based his whole train of thought on the idea that everyone may be entitled to pray but

Who and To Whom

not all prayers are God's children; hence, not everyone praying to God is predestined to enter eternal rest with Him (Christianity.com 2013). TULIP, an acronym to help subjects remember the key principles of John Calvin's doctrine, breaks down these critical messages and perhaps explains who can pray to God the Father.

The "T" in TULIP means "Total Depravity [which] asserts that as a consequence of the fall of man into sin, every person is enslaved to sin. People are not by nature inclined to love God, but rather to serve their own interests and to reject the rule of God (Christianity.com 2013)." In Genesis, the Bible asserts that through the disobedience of Adam and Eve, all men, women included have sinned and will die (Genesis 2:16-17), but only through Jesus, are men redeemed, and saved (1 Corinthians 15:25). Who needs to pray, all men and women, because without Christ, they are enslaved to sin.

The "U" differentiates who can pray and it matters to God. The "U," means:" Unconditional Election [which] asserts that God has chosen from eternity those whom He will bring to be unconditionally grounded in His mercy alone. God has chosen from eternity to extend mercy to those He has chosen and to withhold mercy from those not chosen (Christianity.com 2013)." This frame of mind is supported by the following verse: Romans 9:15, "For he saith to Moses, I will have mercy on whom I will have mercy, and I will have compassion on whom I will have compassion." This nature solely given to God, demonstrates His power, and all-knowing traits to be the perfect judge to determine who may have mercy, who may have His audience, and who can request His ear or simply talk to the elements.

The "L," "Limited Atonement asserts that Jesus's substitutionary atonement was definite and certain in its purpose and in what it accomplished. This implies that only the sins of the elect were atoned for by Jesus's death (Christianity.com 2013)." This conclusion surmised by John Calvin, ruffles many of feathers because it further divides God's people from the world. Yet the Bible states in John 3:16, "For God so loved the world, that he gave his only begotten Son, that whosoever believeth in him should not perish, but have everlasting life."

Yet other scriptures in the Bible say His people are to hate the world (1 John 2:15), even that God is at war with the world (John 15:18-27). A scripture that needs a second read to understand the world in which Jesus was referring to is John 18:36:

"Jesus answered, My kingdom is not of this world: if my kingdom were of this world, then would my servants fight, that I should not be delivered to the Jews: but now is my kingdom not from hence."

This verse would imply, the world spoken about in John 3:16, is not the traditional world as people perceive, but the Kingdom of God.

"I," represents "Irresistible Grace [which] asserts that the saving grace of God is effectually applied to those whom he has determined to save (that is, the elect) and overcomes their resistance to obeying the call of the gospel, bringing them to a saving faith (Christian.com 2013)." This means that when God sovereignly purposes to save someone, that individual certainly will be saved." This presentation of irresistible grace

Who and To Whom

would imply, that those who are saved can pray for others and the Lord hears their prayers. The Bible says in Acts 16:31, "Believe on the Lord Jesus Christ, and you will be saved, you and your household (NKJV)." Christians believe they can pray for the living to be saved, contrary to Catholics who continue to pray for the dead (Catholic News Herald 2019).

The Catholics have a day of prayer for the dead, it is called All Saints Day, and they claim this act is supported by the Catechism, the Church's funeral liturgy, and rooted in Old Testament readings. Calvin was a prophesying Protestant who did not agree with many teachings of the Catholic Church. On this important day for Catholics, they gather in an act of worship, and not merely an expression of grief. It is a time when the Church gathers with the family and friends of the deceased "to give praise and thanks to God for Christ's victory over sin and death, to commend the deceased to God's tender mercy and compassion, and to seek strength in the proclamation of the Paschal Mystery…"

The Catholics emphasize a person cannot pray or have a "Celebration of Life" if they have not yet been raised from the dead. This is also a dividing point between Protestants and Catholics. Protestants who make up a vast denomination registry would agree that once a Christian dies, they enter rest; unless they are not having rest, meaning they are going to hell.

Protestants did not believe in purgatory, paying and praying for the dead to reach heaven after they had left this life (Catholics have since abandoned this theory as well). They also don't gather and continue to pray for the dead as a form of worship, although the dead may be a part of a prayer. To explain, a Catholic is still requesting that the Lord remove sins from the deceased and prepare room for them in heaven. Whereas, the Protestants would say, "Thank you God for making room for our forefathers Abraham and Jacob," and the list would go on and on. There is a difference between praying for the dead and praying about the dead.

In Luke 16:26 it implies once a person dies, they cannot cross back over, and this could be inferred to mean, once a person dies, breathing their last breath, they will be judged. That judgment cannot be overturned like how the fallen angels' judgment cannot be overturned. The Word that comes forth out of the Father's mouth will not turn unto Him void but will accomplish what He sent it out to do (Isiah 55:11).

The final letter, "P," means "Perseverance of the Saints [which] asserts that since God is sovereign and His will cannot be frustrated by humans or anything else, those whom God has called into communion with Himself will continue in faith until the end (Christian.com 2013)." God can sustain anyone in His hands, and no one can pluck that person out (John 10:28). A protestant view on who can pray is not only different than a Catholic but also differs from the Jew and perhaps the Muslim.

The Jew believes the "who," as it pertains to who can pray, and who is listening varies from the Christian, Catholic, or Protestant. Finkelman argues that Jews should not pray to their ancestors or the dead. For example, he writes:

"What about asking my deceased ancestors to plead my

case before God? A familiar Yiddish phrase depends on their having that role, referring to the deceased as a "gebeter" (Hebrew equivalent: meliz tov or meliz yosher), but perhaps we should not ever invoke that phrase. Presumably, asking my ancestors to forgive all my sins and bring redemption to the house of Israel would amount to forbidden ancestor worship (Finkelman 2016-2017:128)."

     He raises the issue of who a Jew should address their prayers to. Can they ask angels and dead ancestors for help? He seems to poke fun at if there is a difference between praying and asking. If prayer simply means to ask, he argues a person should be able to ask anything, like how people ask anything in prayer.

     He further argues, that if prayer is simply asking, why can't someone pray that a waiter, robot, animal, or similar noun absolve sins (Finkelman 2016-2017:128)? He says a request like absolving sins, when asked of God, means prayer and not asking. He says the Jewish penitential prayer Makhnisei Rahamim, a prayer asking for angels to intercede and bring our prayers to God is controversial (Finkelman 2016-2017:128). Perhaps, this is a common thought that the Catholics share with the Jews who do believe praying to an outside influence, hence a being other than God, is okay as long as they are asking for that angel or saint to speak to God for them.

     Finkelman agrees with the Protestants in this relation, in that nothing should intercede for man, but he argues that any prayer has "a touch of idolatry (Finkelman 2016-2017:129)." He explains his logic by writing, "Every petitionary prayer, no matter how pure, has a touch of idolatry since every believing Jew (or Muslim, or other pure monotheist) directs her prayers at God as she conceives of God. In other words, we direct our prayers at the best conception of God that we can manage, which also means, at a somewhat inadequate representation of the infinite (Finkelman 2016-2017:129)."

He sides with "Samuelson who calls this approaching God as an "asymptote" (Samuelson 1993:252) since we can imagine a long curve from abjectly inappropriate conceptions of God to increasingly appropriate conceptions; we can approach closer and closer to and appropriate conception, but we cannot ever achieve the target (129)." This shared thought of not being able to address God the Father, because any way a person tries to approach God, the imagery they see, would likely resemble a human is a parallel to what the Buddhists believe.

The Buddhist do not attempt to assume that there is a supreme being greater than all life but do recognize there are superhumans or things in the atmosphere, but they choose to ignore God and pray to a tangible concept in their mind (Gross 2002:79). Gross writes that "…[this] form found in such Buddhist liturgies is at least superficially similar to many familiar Christian forms of address to the deity, despite the theological differences (Gross 2002:79)."

Knohl, who could share some of the sentiments of Finkelman, in that if a person can imagine, or think of an image of any kind, that is idolatry. He proposes that everybody ought not to pray because they are not aware of whom they pray to. There are rules, regulations, and specifications assigned to those who are

Who and To Whom

supposed to pray, especially as it pertains to the Jew. He argues that if these guidelines are not followed, the Jewish faith would look no different than a pagan religion.

He makes a noteworthy claim in his article Between Voice and Silence, "It is worthy noting the distinction between the circle of the priestly cult (and similar to that of the song of the Levites), which is entirely fixed and obligatory, and that of prayer, which was more on the order of a goodly custom and an act of piety, but did not carry the stamp of fixity and was not understood as an obligation imposed on every person in Israel (Knohl 1996:23)."

He implies not every Jew is required to pray, but the Levite is obligated to pray. He makes a distinction of who must pray and who doesn't have to, and if they do it is simply a custom or act of piety. The Christian in large contrast, requires every believer to pray. The Muslim also believes every believer should pray, however, the Mu'adhdhin is the one that gives the prayer call, adhan. Not just anybody can give this call, but a special servant leads the call and the prayer.

The audience to whom the Muslims speak is Allah. There is debate between many on whether Allah is the same God as the Christians, or if he is a god. This book on prayer does not attempt to present information on whether either is true but demonstrates the variations on who can pray and to whom they believe they pray. An additional group that must be spoken about, are the groups that don't identify or are not categorized as Christian.

A question Fidelis Nkomazana asks in his writing Missionary Colonial Mentality and the Expansion of Christianity in Bechuanaland Protectorate (Botswana), 1800 to 1900, is, can Christians and non-Christians pray to the same God using different names? Many may argue they understand the parallel between the Muslim, Jew, and Christian, but what about cultures who don't or didn't use the name God, Jesus, or Allah, can their prayers be understood as one to the Divine, or do they automatically go into the pagan category despite the claim to a monotheistic viewpoint?

He writes about the culture present in the country before the missionaries and he says, "Batswana traditionally believed in a single Supreme Being whom they called Modimo, literally meaning the one who is supreme and above. Modimo was believed to be the Creator, Maker, Originator, and Source of all things including life (Willoughby 1969: 80; Schapera 1961:63). The word Modimo has always denoted a single Supreme Being. Wherever the word is used to denote an ancestor or a spirit of the dead or a living person whom one honors greatly, the word modimo (with a lowercase 'm,' a singular word for badimo) is used."

This concept can be understood through a Christian, Catholic, and Protestant lens without much effort. We understand the use of "god" and "God." Muslims choose not to call Allah god/God because they believe that is a word that can apply to too many beings. Hence a little "g" or the big "G," so they don't use the word God at all. A similar finding can also be said about the words "Lord," "Elohim," and "Adoni;" this time even a Jew can relate.

So if all these faiths can use a word and understand to whom is being addressed, why did the mis-

Who and To Whom

sionaries feel their interpretation of who God is, as far as their given names was superior to another culture? The missionaries called their ceremonies in which a rain-maker, a tribal leader, would pray for the harvest pagan, sinister, or evil. But Nkomazana argues, that they only judged what they attempted not to understand, in that, the rain-maker prayed to Modimo as the Creator and sustainer of all forms of life, and the dance in his opinion would appear no different than how David danced, or how both Christians and Jews pray for the harvest (Nkomazana 2015:31).

A question that must be asked is who can judge another person's prayers, or determine to whom their prayers are directed. Christians, Jews, and Muslims, the top three monotheistic opinions would agree, that the Bible was provided to demonstrate God's character. If one wants to know who God is, to determine if they are praying to Him, or another that person could study the character of the one to which they pray. It can be argued, using Paul as an example, when he told the Corinthians, the statue they had of the unknown "God," is in fact the only true God. Perhaps, if Paul were to examine, the character of Modimo, would he determine they know God like he did, but knew Him by a different name, or determine they were pagans, heathens?

There appear to be rules as to who can pray, for example, the atheist cannot pray. They cannot pray because they don't believe, nor see the purpose of praying if they are talking to no one or nothing. Unlike how the atheist doesn't pray, the Buddhists, although they believe there are supernatural beings, feel there is not one supreme being; yet they pray. The Jews, Christians, and Muslims all pray, but they differ on who can pray and I would suggest how to pray.

"How to Pray"

Traditions are what is believed to keep a family unified through the ages. This common thought for many, is no different than what many faiths believe must be in place to uphold their core values juxtaposed to society, other religious thoughts, and practices happening around them. Zev Gotthold believes prayer is the strongest unifying factor in the survival of Jewish communities (Gotthold 1961:107). He further explains,

"The unifying language of our prayers has, by itself, often helped to make for intelligible contact between Jews of entirely different backgrounds and mother tongues. Our liturgy has not only been a way of Jewish expression but has also to a large extent impressed upon us common theological and national ideas that have made for a feeling of solidarity and belongingness amongst Jews who otherwise might have been strangers to each other (Gotthold 1961:107)."

Jewish culture argues that prayer is the bedrock for tying their people together and maintaining their traditions, separating them from other whites (Leonard 2007:152). Without vision, some may argue that people perish (Proverbs 29:18), because of the thought, that man must train up a child in the direction they should go (Proverbs 22:6). If there is the need to study to show oneself approved (2 Timothy 2:15) or to train up a child, there has to be a standard, a tradition arguable, one must learn and follow to arrive especially pertaining to one's belief maturation.

In the article by Zev Gotthold, Tradition: A Journal of Orthodox Jewish Thought, he argues that the young Jew must learn the traditional prayers, say the traditional prayers, and speak in Hebrew, because there is intrinsic value to doing so. He argues much is lost for those who have to temporize with translations (Gotthold 1961:108). He further notes, that the uprising of youth synagogues that are unaffiliated with parent churches, is perpetuating a melting pot approach to prayer and tradition. He says, "Sometimes, though, there are endeavors to preserve cultural values that have survived with some communities for millennia and which are now threatened with extinction (Gotthold 1961:109)."

With the onset of name it and claim it doctrine flooding the church, the original heartbeat, traditions of praying for the nations, salvation, and forgiveness of sins have been eclipsed to praying for one's own family; then further limited to somebody they know instead of the prayer being intended to cover Kingdom believers (Baker 2008:178). During the Conference on Uniform Prayer held January 4, 1961, Dr. Chouraqui voiced the demand that people who live together and work together must also worship together, praying to the God

How to Pray

of our common ancestors in the same sacred tongue (Gotthold 1961:110)." If this ideology is to be applied to all believers, the Black church may have a point to ask the question, is it possible for whites, the descendants of the Masters who enslaved their ancestors, to pray and worship together?

In an article published by American Magazine, the evidence would point to a dream undesired by Rev. Martin Luther King Jr. Although the film "Selma" was nominated for an Oscar, it would appear most Americans, predominantly white Americans are okay with integration as it pertains to politics and business, but believe it is not necessary for the church pew (Grossman 2015).

To further explain, "People like the idea of diversity. They just don't like being around different people," said Ed Stetzer in the article. The survey conducted on 1,000 Americans, had this to report:

* 67 percent say their church has done enough to become more ethnically diverse.

* 40 percent want to see more diversity.

* 71 percent of evangelicals say their church is diverse enough.

* Race and ethnicity reveal sharp differences. Only 37 percent of whites want their church to be more diverse, compared to 47 percent of Hispanic Americans and 51 percent of African Americans.

*Among 1,000 American adults, 82 percent say diversity is good for the country — but not necessarily in their church pews.

* Of the 34 percent of Americans who say they have worshipped regularly where they were a minority, one in five of them said their minority status hindered their involvement.

* 22 percent have never experienced being a minority at church, but they think it would make them uncomfortable.

* There's not much urgency about diversity. Half of those surveyed think the churches are "too segregated," but 44 percent disagree.

*The survey of 1,000 Protestant senior pastors found that 43 percent say they speak about racial reconciliation once a year or less.

Perhaps the findings demonstrate why it is hard for people of different cultural backgrounds to pray together because how each group prays varies in what they pray about and ask for. The largest churches amongst the Black church, are Baptist, Methodist, and Protestant denominations, yet many if not all, separate themselves from white counterparts on the week-to-week schedule. They attend conferences together and listen to the same gospel, but it would appear they relate very differently.

The Jews like the Blacks who started the African Methodist Church, attempt to separate themselves from "whites" and their social practices to protect their culture and livelihood, shielding them from racism or grouping them with persons that do not like them

How to Pray
(Ame-church.com 2019, Leonard 2007:155).

An analysis by Rabbi Elimelekh Bar-Shaul mentions the moral justification for demanding cultural and religious integration, but, even from the purely cultural point of view, utterly rejected the concept of melting-pot fusion (Gotthold 1961:111). He doesn't believe this integration should be forced, nor should it focus on pushing young Jews to follow specific traditions, but believes the church should focus on re-establishing the Tabernacle as a place they (young/youth Jews) can take refuge and satisfy their emotional needs (Gotthold 1961:111). He desires for the government and other Rabbis to not focus on how Jews pray, in that, they should have "the same freedom of expression to religious worship that is granted to art and literature, where the government has made no attempt to act as leveler and homogenizer (Gotthold 1961:111)." In the Jewish faith, the church leaders feel very compelled to control or teach their people how to pray.

Rituals, Traditions, Vs. the Heart of Prayer

In addition to knowing the prayers the person has to understand, although the tradition is important, it must not circumvent the Word, command of God, or that tradition is not of God but of men. To understand the value of any tradition, knowing why a certain thing is a tradition must be understood. In Mark 7, the Pharisees and scribes (Jewish elders) ask Jesus why his disciples did not wash their hands before they ate. He responded to them:

6 He answered and said unto them, Well hath Esaias (Isaiah) prophesied of you hypocrites, as it is

written, These people honoureth me with their lips, but their heart is far from me.

7 Howbeit in vain do they worship me, teaching for doctrines the commandments of men.

8 For laying aside the commandment of God, ye hold the tradition of men, as the washing of pots and cups: and many other such like things ye do.

9 And he said unto them, Full well ye reject the commandment of God, that ye may keep your own tradition.

10 For Moses said, Honour thy father and thy mother; and, Whoso curseth father or mother, let him die the death:

11 But ye say, If a man shall say to his father or mother, It is Corban, that is to say, a gift, by whatsoever thou mightest be profited by me; he shall be free.

12 And ye suffer him no more to do ought for his father or his mother;

13 Making the word of God of none effect through your tradition, which ye have delivered: and many such like things do ye.

Verse 6 and 8, speaks of how the Pharisees can do physical actions, hence perform rituals, but like is written in 9 they reject the command of God; and by extension make the rituals, the things God said to do bend to their own tradition instead of follow His meaning. They were to wash their hands and perform these deeds to realize why they were not clean, they were not internally good, but they needed to perform these acts because it was to be done unto the Lord and not unto their own righteousness.

The commands God gave for them to follow, the way they were to live, they rejected, and they changed the meaning of why they do a thing, and when that happened they didn't realize they lost sight of God altogether. To follow a tradition, or perform a ritual lacking the understanding, relationship, heart, and connection with God, makes the ritual itself nothing more than an action being performed.

When David ate the shewbread from the temple and shared it with his men because the priest gave it to him, he did not bring disgrace upon himself, or condemnation to his men, nor the priest because he was following the command of the Father (1 Samuel 21:6, Matt 12:4). Although the Jews had the actions right, their hearts were far from God. Like the verses, the Jews were great at saying and praying the right things to hear, but their hearts were far from God's purpose. This truth is also spoken of in Revelation as it pertains to His churches and their desires to serve their own desires. A follow-up question would arise, "Do people pray the prayers God wants them to, or the ones they want to?"

Knohl who is a strong advocate for following tradition, must also realize the Levites themselves did not follow the Law of the Sabbath. In Matt 12:5 Jesus points out, "Or haven't you read in the Law that on the Sabbath the priests in the temple break the Sabbath and yet are innocent?" They break the Law by working on the Sabbath, but they are innocent because they are following God's command over the tradition, and obedience is greater than sacrifice (1 Samuel 15:22, Mark 7:7).

As it pertains to how to pray, Knohl writes: "As has been noted by scholars, the people were accustomed to reciting their own prayers at the time of offering the daily sacrifice and the burning of the incense. The Temple may therefore be described as a series of concentric circles. The inner circle is that of the priests, in which the sacred service is conducted in absolute silence; the outer circle is that of the folk prayers of the people; while in the middle is the circle of the song of the Levites (Knohl 1996:23)."

He further writes, during the Day of Atonement, "The holy prayer uttered inside the Temple was that of the high priest…But that even this prayer is not conducted in the holiest place of all…The priest recites his prayer only after he has completed the sanctified ritual and left the holy of holies (Knohl 1996:23)."

It would appear a lot of instruction for how to pray coincides with rituals. Some may interpret that to mean traditional behaviors, but what happens when the New Testament states there is no longer a need for these sacrifices because Jesus paid it all? If he fulfilled the law (Matthew 5:17-20, Hebrews 10:1-18), how then is a Jew supposed to pray, if they are not willing to give up the rituals? The holies of holies where only a select few were permitted, now, the Christian believes they may all go boldly to the throne of grace, before God, and make their prayers known (Hebrews 4:16).

A few more examples Knohl attempts to make to support his argument prayer should be done in

How to Pray

silence, by the educated, trained, or priestly, which may imply pastors and those called spiritual leaders that also believe in the God of the Jew.

"In one baraita in which the sages discuss the laws of prayer, they attempt to find precedent in the behavior of biblical personalities: "Shall it be that he makes his voice heard in prayer? It is expounded regarding Hannah: "Hannah spoke in her heart. These remarks are rather surprising: from what may be inferred from the biblical text, it would seem that prayer recited aloud was the accepted practice during the biblical period, whereas Hannah's practice was the exception, as indicated by Eli's suspicions: "Therefore Eli took her to be a drunken woman (1 Sam 1:13)." Why then did the sages see fit to decree that the Amida prayer be recited in silence, based on the singular case of Hannah, as opposed to the usual practice of prayer recited aloud, as suggested by numerous biblical passages and the literature of the Second Temple period (Knohl 1996:27)?"

His argument, is why would prayers be traditionally recited silently if vocal, praying out loud, were more common than silent prayer? He further explains it may be suitable for confessions to be recited silently, but he argues that prayers of worship should be done in a quiet whisper (Knohl 1996:26). The Catholics can identify with the ritual of select clergy performing certain tasks for Mass.

How the priest is the main focus for certain rituals to be performed and how he is entrusted to pray over the congregation and during the service while many of the participants remain silent. Confession is also done in a whisper, although it is about one person reporting to the priest, but like in the example of Hannah, Eli sent Hannah away and said she would have what she asked for. Is not the priest suggesting the same, "Your sins are forgiven" or if he says "You have what you ask?"

The Protestant faith is one that would turn this entire situation around and focus on the battle of Jericho as to how they pray. The story in Joshua 6 talks about a city with walls thicker than 4.9 to 6.6 ft and taller than 28ft. The task to take the city would seem impossible, but God was on their side. He simply told them to walk about the building with the ark, and at a given time they were to shout, and the walls would come tumbling down.

Often in Black gospel songs, in sermon messages, and in prayer, many shout with the voice of triumph in the black church (Psalm 47:1). In the Christian faith, a person's faith is voiced even at times to everyone listening by way of giving a testimony. For the salvation prayer, many stand before a congregation to commit their life to God. This confession is not in a whisper, but projected on microphones or shouted out in a voice for everyone to hear.

Another example where Knohl points to scripture to define how prayer ought to work that may draw differences across Judaism, Catholicism, and Protestant faiths, is his evaluation of the communication, prayer, and speaking, between Moses and God. He claims, "Moreover, in the work of this school there is no connection of direct speech between God and Israel; only Moses himself hears God's word. Indeed, even the verbal connection with Moses is one-sided; God turns

How to Pray

to Moses and speaks to him, but there is no speech of Moses to God! (Knohl 1996:20)."

Catholics would embrace the theory that God only speaks to a select few, to be more specific the pope or high official of the church. In the beginning of the church and perhaps the sentiments still remain, God doesn't use everyone to speak His Word; nor does He entrust everyone to be His personification on earth. During sacraments the Catholics perform, they believe they are the reincarnated Christ on earth when they perform these rituals.

They believe the pope, priest, is above regular men/women to the extent the pope is deemed infallible. To imply there is a man without sin, would contradict scripture, the Word of God, which says all men have fallen short of the glory of God (Romans 3:23). This tradition or ideology would seem to be a tradition of men rather than of God based on scripture from the book they all share.

The Protestants would strongly disagree that communicating with God is one-sided. They would point to the burning bush, in which Moses had a conversation with God. They would point to the prayers he made before God, raising his complaint that he didn't speak well enough to communicate God's message before the pharaoh; and perhaps Aaron needs to serve. That conversation is recorded below:

10 "And Moses said unto the LORD, O my LORD, I am not eloquent, neither heretofore, nor since thou hast spoken unto thy servant: but I am slow of speech, and of a slow tongue.

11 And the LORD said unto him, Who hath made man's mouth? or who maketh the dumb, or deaf, or the seeing, or the blind? Have not I the LORD?

12 Now therefore go, and I will be with thy mouth, and teach thee what thou shalt say (Exodus 4:10-12)."

Christians, especially Protestants, believe prayer is done with communication back and forth between man and God. When Jesus tore the veil, he reestablished a connection between every man and God. Anyone now can come to God, without the help of a priest or rabbi, and make their request known unto God. As believed by them, they can be whispered, shouted, spoken, or be formed in one's thoughts (Psalms 139:2); because the Lord can receive them all.

The Muslim perhaps can also relate to silent prayers, as much of the Muslim prayer, salat, is done in a small voice. There was and perhaps still is an ongoing debate as to what parts of the prayer should be silent, and which read aloud. Naseer Ahlmad Faruqui seems to agree that Bayan al-Quran had the right explanation for why the prayer should be done in both respects:

"It means that neither should the whole recitation of the Salat be uttered loudly, nor should it be all uttered silently, but the middle course should be taken i.e., some part of the Salat should be uttered aloud so that the whole congregation should be alike in rendering obeisance to the Might and Majesty of Allah, and some part should be silent so that each member of the congregation remembers Allah in his own way (aaiil.org 1984)."

How to Pray

The Christian, both Catholic and Protestant could agree that prayer is to be made silent and aloud in different settings to impress different meanings when someone is praying. Elizabeth Brummel, in the article You Don't Have to Pray to Somebody in Special English': Style, Narration, and Salvation in Urban Kenya, her interview with Joshua points to the idea that prayer and sermons are best understood when it is made personal (Brummel 2014:265). Understanding scriptures and sermon messages, one typically puts oneself in the person's shoes in order to make the story personally identifiable, reflecting almost a communication between God and the recipient.

Another common thread between the Jews, Muslims, and Catholics are prayer books. These three faiths have prayers that are traditional for certain holidays, events, and celebrations. The Protestant Christian may have a few celebrations like communion where a specific prayer is offered, however, that prayer is not pre-written to where everyone says it the exact same way, but it has the same meaning. Sure, there are books published about prayers one can pray in the Christian faith, but none of them are the affixed way to prayer, except for the Lord's Prayer. This prayer is read straight from the Bible and the understanding is universal in the Protestant church from white to black church or other.

Prayer Examples

The Lord's Prayer reads as follows and this marks a guide for how Christians, perhaps predominantly in the Protestant faith give prayers to God as recorded in Matthew 6:9.

9 "After this manner therefore pray ye:
"'Our Father which art in heaven,
hallowed be thy name.
10 Thy kingdom come,
Thy will be done in earth,
as it is in heaven.
11 Give us this day our daily bread.
12 And forgive us our debts,
 as we forgive our debtors.
13 And lead us not into temptation,
but deliver us from evil:
For thine is the kingdom,
and the power, and the glory, forever. Amen

Here is a quick list of how to read each phrase from the Lord's Prayer. The first line starts with:

- "Our Father which art in heaven," Our Father, represents His deity, dominion, and position in a believer's life. To use the word Father suggests an intimate relationship and authority that God has over a life, calling Him Father pays reverence. For everyone that doesn't call him, Father signifies they do not reverence Him as that.

1 Corinthians 8:6, AMP says, "Yet for us, there is but one God, the Father, who is the source of all things, and we exist for Him; and one Lord, Jesus Christ, by whom are all things [that have been created], and we [believers exist and have life and have been redeemed] through Him". This shows that those who receive His son Jesus Christ become children of God. Which art in heaven speaks of His residence and rule. The Lord

How to Pray

is above and not beneath, He speaks of His eminent domain in Ephesians 4:6.

- "Hallowed be thy name." According to Dictionary.com, hallowed is a synonym for holy. His name is sacred. Acknowledging who The Lord is—gives Him reverence for being great. Psalm 24:8 states, "Who is this King of glory? The Lord strong and mighty, The Lord mighty in battle."

To explain, people don't speak when the judge is talking nor show any disrespect because it would not be tolerated. An officer is there to enforce the judge's strongest power to impose sanctions for acts of disruptions, either fines or jail. Jesus and the angels, fallen or still dwelling in heaven, are under God's wise control (Jude 1:25).

- "Thy kingdom come," Is acknowledging His heavenly authority with control over believers and their presence in the world. Kingdom can be broken down into two words, king and dom (meaning domain). A king is an individual who rules his kingdom or multiple domains. The domain is a territory governed by a single ruler. Thy (or) king is God, the kingdom and domain are both ruled by Him.

Hebrews 13:14, YLT confirms, "For we have not here an abiding city, but the coming one we seek"; along with Rev. 11:15 that reads, "And the seventh angel sounded; and there were great voices in heaven, saying, The kingdoms of this world are become the kingdoms of our Lord, and of his Christ; and he shall reign forever and ever." This is declaring the functions of God's domain be done on earth.

- "Thy will be done in earth, as it is in heaven." Believers should desire to submit to God's rule on earth and demonstrate His will for others to see. According to Romans 12:1-2, AMP a believer should live by this saying and their prayers should be synonymous with the concept:

"Therefore I urge you, brothers and sisters, by the mercies of God, to present your bodies [dedicating all of yourselves, set apart] as a living sacrifice, holy and well-pleasing to God, which is your rational (logical, intelligent) act of worship. And do not be conformed to this world [any longer with its superficial values and customs], but be transformed and progressively changed [as you mature spiritually] by the renewing of your mind [focusing on godly values and ethical attitudes], so that you may prove [for yourselves] what the will of God is, that which is good and acceptable and perfect [in His plan and purpose for you]."

Another suitable verse to discuss is Daniel 2:44 which reads, "And in the days of these kings shall the God of heaven set up a kingdom, which shall never be destroyed: and the kingdom shall not be left to other people, but it shall break in pieces and consume all these kingdoms, and it shall stand forever."

- "Give us this day our daily bread." Daily bread is a metaphor for immediate needs or simply what people need every day to survive. Here, the person initiating prayer is asking for God's strength, food, and other must-haves to sustain daily life. This request focuses on a 24-hour period, because believers are told to focus on today, for tomorrow will take care of itself (Matt 6:34).

How to Pray

The Hebrews were told that God provided manna from heaven, only to take what is needed for that day because He will provide again tomorrow (Exodus 16:4-21). If more was gathered, it was expected that the extra would be shared among those who needed it. Any amount left over by morning would spoil. This was also requested to keep people from laziness in seeking God and trusting His provision for the day. Prayer should contain requests, concerned with the individual's daily needs. Yes, God knows the need before anyone prays, but He wants to hear, feel, and see trust by believers relying on Him for provision.

- "And forgive us our debts, as we forgive our debtors." Forgiveness may be difficult for many, especially when someone has done catastrophic or unimaginable things to a person, but it's divine to forgive for Christ's sake. Believers are called to extend forgiveness fully and freely towards those who have hurt them. Who can stand before God and ask for pardon if they haven't first forgiven those they can see (1 John 4:20)? Ephesians 4:31-32 reminds people, "Let all bitterness, and wrath, and anger, and clamor, and evil speaking, be put away from you, with all malice: And be ye kind one to another, tenderhearted, forgiving one another, even as God for Christ's sake hath forgiven you."

- "And lead us not into temptation," said, Professor D. A. Carson, from Trinity Seminary in Chicago, that Jesus is using a figure of speech for The Lord's Prayer called litotes, which expresses something positive by negating its opposite. For example, if one says, "This is no small matter," rather than "It is a big matter." When praying, "lead us not into temptation," it is a plea to "Keep me from being ensnared by temptation."

In short, the prayer is asking, "Lord, don't let Satan ambush me. Don't let the enemies of my soul catch me in their trap. Reserve them in chains of darkness." The confidence in praying this verse is acknowledging that God has the power to lead one past all lures of temptation that threaten them.

- "But deliver us from evil:" Evil recognizes its power for tempting Christians to partake and even invite immorality, but this line is an appeal to God for His protection. The devil tried to tempt Jesus to worship him, and he said in return "…Get thee behind me, Satan; for it is written, Thou shalt worship the Lord thy God, and him only shalt thou serve (Luke 4:8)."

The last section of The Lord's Prayer asks for the ability not to sin and receive deliverance from evil. Unlike the movies popular in Hollywood, Christians acknowledge the devil is not dressed in a red suit, but he represents levels of darkness and strategies for atrocious things as described in Ephesians 6:12. The devil tempts man by attempting to lure them to his lies, and make them doubters of God and God's power (Genesis 3:4). Non-praying Christians are believed to be weak in the faith, poor in spirit, and unable to stay awake to perceive danger like the disciples who kept falling asleep when asked by Christ to watch and pray (Matthew 26:41).

"For thine is the kingdom, and the power, and the glory, forever. Amen." His domain, qualification, and distinction, are confirmed in 1 Chronicles 29:11 which reads, "Thine, O LORD is the greatness, and the

How to Pray

power, and the glory, and the victory, and the majesty: for all that is in the heaven and in the earth is thine; thine is the kingdom, O LORD, and thou art exalted as head above all."

In understanding the Lord's Prayer, a popular prayer that has made its way into the Catholic church and the Buddhist meditation is the Serenity prayer. The Serenity Prayer reads as follows, "God, grant me the serenity to accept what I cannot change, the courage to change what I can, and the wisdom to know the difference." The Buddhist version reads, "Grant me the serenity to accept what I cannot change, the courage to change what I can, and the wisdom to know the difference."

The saying was originally coined by Reinhold Niebuhr, a member of the Catholic Church (Shapiro 2014). The saying was highly publicized when alcoholic anonymous began using the prayer for recovering attics. This short, yet powerful prayer, is asking God to help the person know what they can do. Give them the ability to do it, then if there is nothing the person can do, accept that, and if possible trust God to change it.

The Buddhists love prayer for an entirely different reason (Gross 2002:77). The Buddhists believe God is only as real as they imagine, and without their imagination, He (God) doesn't exist or is not relevant. So the ability to pray without asking for the fulfillment of this prayer to be performed by God, hence, He is not included, is in essence, the Buddhist praying to a deeper consciousness, perhaps can be inferred as positive self-talk, motivation, to help their mind get on with their daily habits. The prayer for the Christian, or recovering alcoholic is much the same, a request for daily provision, like the Lord's Prayer is for the Protestant believer, and salat made by the Muslim.

Body Language

In understanding how to pray, an important factor that cannot be overlooked that contributes to the experience is posture or body language. For example, when making salat, the Muslim has to face Mecca. Huda explains the process in his article, Marking the Qiblah Facing Makkah (Meeca) for Muslim Prayer. He writes:

"The Qiblah refers to the direction that Muslims face when engaged in ritual prayer. Wherever they are in the world, guttural Muslims are instructed to face Makka (Mecca) in modern-day Saudi Arabia. Or, more technically, Muslims are to face the Ka'aba--the sacred cubic monument that is found in Makka.
The Arabic word Qiblah comes from a root word (Q-B-L) meaning "to face, confront, or encounter" something. It is pronounced "qib" guttural Q sound) and "la." The word rhymes with 'bib-la (Huda 2019).'"

The Catholics had a formation and taught many nations how to pray. Many of the early missionaries to Africa were French Catholics. It is often said, the Catholics taught people to bow their heads and close their eyes, because while a person wasn't looking, they would remove items, or steal, from their congregation. Nkomazna points to an African saying, "When the white man came to our country he had the Bible and we had the land. The white man said to us: 'Let us pray.' After the prayer the white man had the land and we had the Bible (Dube 200:3) (Nkomazna 2015:40)."

How to Pray

Although, this may be a political way of understanding prayer as it pertains to Catholics, purgatory, the ability to pray for the dead and pay them out of hell was an intimidating pressure put on the poor. Many people gave their last to the church believing their money and prayers, helped their ancestors rest in peace. Many called this act a sham, Martin Luther judged the church for antics like this and became a pioneer for the Protestant movement. This one action was not what solely kicked the separation from Catholics to Protestants, the biggest difference was on how the two prayed.

The Catholic Church was heavily influenced by Constantine, a known pagan who attempted to merge Christian principles with his current beliefs. He attempted a fusion of the religions to appease his people, but many would argue such fusion changed the message of God (Revelation 3:15-17). The EAEC published an article that says the following:

"Constantine's emphasis on making his newfound Christianity palatable to the heathen in the Empire, the "Christianization" of these pagan deities was facilitated. For example, pagan rituals and idols gradually took on Christian meanings and names and were incorporated into "Christian" worship (e.g., "saints" replaced the cult of pagan gods in both worship and as patrons of cities; mother/son statues were renamed Mary and Jesus; etc.) and pagan holidays were reclassified as Christian holy days (e.g., The Roman Lupercalia and the feast of purification of Isis became the Feast of the Nativity; the Saturnalia celebrations were replaced by Christmas celebrations; and ancient festival of the dead was replaced by All Souls Day, rededicated to

Christian heroes [now Halloween]. A transition had occurred – instead of being persecuted for failure to worship pagan deities, Christians who did not agree with the particular orthodoxy backed by the Emperor were now persecuted in the name of Christ (EAEC.org 2019!"

In light of this history, the understanding of how Catholics pray may be closer align to how a pagan would pray. The Catholic missionaries had the easiest time to convert the LoDagaa tribe. A tribe located in Ghana, because they told the people that they didn't have to give up their religious thoughts, but make a conversion, hence adopting Christian names for their already defined deities (Hawkins 1997:52).

The missionaries wished this same relationship was found with the people of Botswana who were solely focused on Modimo. They even called the Christian God Modimo against the wishes of the Catholics to call Him Momio (Nkomazana 2015:36,37). To outline the correlation, of what this article refers to as a 'cult,' it writes out the difference between a Catholic prayer and a Protestant prayer.

"1. In 'The Holy Father's Prayer for the Marian Year [1987],' John Paul II asks Mary to do what only God can do – comfort, guide, strengthen, and protect "the whole of humanity ..." His prayer ends: "Sustain us, O Virgin Mary, on our journey of faith and obtain for us the grace of eternal salvation." (4/97, Berean Call).

2. In preparing for an expected earthquake in December 1990, in the Saint Louis area, parishioners at St. Agatha RC church turned to St. Agatha, "the patron

How to Pray

saint of protection from the devastation of volcanoes, earthquakes, fire, and all kinds of violence." The church reported in the St. Louis Southwest City Journal of 10/21/90 that a novena was to be held, including a recitation of the rosary, a prayer to St. Agatha, and a closing benediction. (Reported in the November/December 1990, Foundation.)

3.	A Roman Catholic ritual for selling a home: Put a statue of St. Joseph in a bottle or mason jar and bury it in the front yard (head first), thereby guaranteeing a quick sale of the home. After the sale, the seller is to dig up St. Joseph, put him in a prominent place in the new residence, and pray to him (Mother Angelica, EWTN Catholic TV, 10/95).

Take note in the following two prayers how Mary is magnified above Jesus...

o	Hail Mary full of grace, the Lord is with thee. Blessed art thou among women and blessed is the fruit of thy womb, Jesus. Holy Mary, mother of God, pray for us sinners, now and at the hour of our death. Amen. Why is Mary being prayed to this way, is she God? The Bible never directs us to pray to Mary.

o	"Hail, holy Queen, Mother of Mercy! Our life, our sweetness and our hope! To thee do we cry, poor banished children of Eve. To thee do we send up our sighs, mourning and weeping, in this valley of tears. Turn, then, most gracious Advocate, thine eyes of mercy toward us; and after this our exile show unto us the blessed fruit of thy womb, Jesus. O clement, O loving, O sweet Virgin Mary." Roman Catholicism should be renamed "Mary Worship", because that is really what it is; it places her on a high pedestal, equal with God.

Mary was the mother of Jesus, nothing more, and she is not the advocate as mentioned in the Bible (1 John 2:1)."

In light of these fundamental findings, it would appear, that Catholics pray to Saint Mary, regard the pope as God incarnate through transubstantiation, and believe that repetition sayings such as "Hail Mary" are enough to request forgiveness of sin. The Bible speaks against repetitious babblings and considers such speech in a prayer to God unsatisfying because they are pagan prayers and do not fit petitions for the Creator of all life (Matthew 6:7).

Protestants also do not direct their prayers to anyone except God, and Jesus is included to close the prayer, but they do not pray to saints, nor do they pray to statues, images, or pictures of Jesus. They reject the doctrine of transubstantiation, as no man can be the personified Great I AM, and they do not keep relics or idols as to have them is taboo and would be likened to voodoo.

Inside many Christian churches with a Protestant denomination, you will seldom find statues of Mary, saints, and as of late pictures or statues of the crucifixion of Christ. Many Black churches shifted away from the white Jesus pictures, and although some replaced the pictures with a black Jesus, many have done away with the imagery altogether.

So what body language do people typically use when they pray, no matter if they pray to God, Allah, or statues? There are three postures that Jurgen Moltmann points out which are: "1. In Islam, worshippers prostrate themselves. 2. Christians fold their hands, close their eyes, and kneel down. 3. The early Christians stood upright in an attitude of adoration, with raised head, open eyes, and outspread arms (Moltmann 1997:93)."

The posture the Muslim takes, and any person that lies prostrate, which also includes Christians that lay before God, are attempting to make themselves as small as possible (Moltmann 1997:93). The person praying is putting themselves in total submission to the one they beseech, and as such is "reminiscent of the vassal's subservience before the absolute power of an Asiatic despot. The vassal threw himself on his face before the ruler, presenting his unprotected neck for execution or pardon, and making himself as small as possible (Moltmann 1997:93)."

"The [second] Christian posture in prayer in the Western church may also have developed out of gestures of political subservience in Germanic culture, although we may presume that Roman culture put a stronger impress on the church in Western Europe, and the hierarchical church evoked its own gestures of subservience (Moltmann 1997:94)."

This prayer position also suggests a powerless individual in need of the Almighty's influence. The third position is one of adoration and expectation from a person ready to embrace the Lord's presence or gifts he explains. Other body language that is suggested by scripture and the interpretation include the following:

- Bowing:

This is an attitude of gratefulness and reverence. Reading Genesis 24:52 Abraham's servant "worshiped the Lord, bowing himself to the earth."

- Hands Raised / Spread:

This is submission or surrendering, a means of non-verbal communication as 1 Timothy 2:8 demonstrates. Similarly, when an officer of the law asks a command from someone to freeze and put their hands up, it is to demonstrate the person is surrendering and poses no threat.

- Kneeling:

This is also a sign of submission, that shows yielding to an authority. This was used by King Solomon to appeal for mercy in 1 Kings 18:41-46.

- Leaping:

Is an action word, that means to act or move hastily or abruptly. This is a form of rejoicing according to Luke 6:23.

- Looking Up to Heaven:

David said in Psalm 121:1-2 that he lifted up his eyes towards the hill. This action of looking directs the eyes towards someone or something for redemption and strength.

- Lying Prostrate:

Is lying down in the lowest position to display humility. This form was displayed by Abraham in Genesis 17:1-22. He "fell on his face" to demonstrate worthlessness and a sign of respect.

- Meditation:

Time set aside to think deeply or focus on God as Psalm 1:2. In doing this, it causes someone to be at peace keeping their mind on The Lord as Isaiah 26:3.

How to Pray

- Sitting:

Paul wrote to encourage saints that sitting in certain seats has authority (Ephesians 2:6.) Sitting at the end of a rectangle table is usually left for the most powerful or influential person. This verse reminds saints they sit with Jesus Christ in heavenly places when accepting Him as Lord.

- Standing:

Is an upright position that is taken when willing to perform an action. Ephesians 6:13-18, It explains an individual preparing for battle or taking a stance on ideology. Like a popular saying, "If you don't stand for something, you'll fall for anything."

- Walking:

Demonstrates a form of moving from one position to another. 1 John 1:5-7 reminds people to move towards the light of God and not darkness. Walking should be in the direction of looking more like Jesus Christ.

- Watching:

This means to be alert, look attentively, or pay close attention. Matthew 26:41 advises people to do this so they don't fall into temptation.

- Dancing:

Rhythmic movement with or without music being performed can also be to an instrument or band of musicians. "Then Miriam the prophetess... took a tambourine in her hand and all the women went out after her with the tambourines in round dances (Exodus 15:20)."

Dancing is a form of prayer or worship, that many prayers can relate to. From the pagans to the Jews, or Christians, dancing is a form of praying and worshiping a deity. As spoken about by Moltmann, there may appear to be a time to dance for some and others to refrain.

"To dance before the gods, in order to give them pleasure and to find pleasure in the gods oneself, is a general practice in all cultic religions. We can still see this today from the temple dancers in India and the dance demonstrations in Africa. Israel, too, danced its experiences of God…But the people also danced round the Golden Calf, until Moses destroyed this image of power (Exodus 32:19) (Moltmann 1997:97)."

Prayer although it may be completed using one or multiple how-to steps, one thing is certain, the heart, ritual, body language, or verbal cues silent or aloud impact prayer. What Joshua explains,

"I came to realize you don't have to pray to somebody in special English, bombastic words and whatever. No. If this person is to get saved, even a single word he will speak, even how broken it is, this person will change his life (Brummel 2014:252)." Contrary to Gross who writes, the power of symbolic, poetic, passionate, and intimate language; and the effectiveness of emotions for transforming consciousness—results in the skillful means of 'prayers' … (Gross 2002:85)."

Some prayers, perhaps better coined as meditational sayings, no matter how eloquent cannot substitute prayers for salvation, atonement, or redemption; although they may work for motivation and thinking

How to Pray

higher of oneself. Prayer doesn't have to have a specific language but the intentions, heart, mind, body, and soul have to be committed. Any of the combinations that can be formed from the list suggested, can bring a person closer to God's heart, or function as a ritual one performs, reduced to mean nothing more than an action one does like an automation system if a piece of this equation is left out or misinterpreted. Knowing how to pray is only a start to knowing when and why to pray.

TC Martin

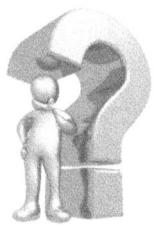

"When and Why Pray"

A popular saying perhaps coined by Christians, all times is the right time to pray. Is there a better understanding of what times are meaningful times to pray? Are there special festivals, events, dates, or even hours that could impact a person's prayer?

There are special events set aside for the Jews, Muslims, Christians, pagans, and sorcerers to pray or perform rites. For the Jew, a special celebration specific to praying where all Jews come together to pray, including celebrity and socially important Jews as well without partiality, is Yom Kippur. A brief understanding of Yom Kippur is outlined on the Israel Ministry of Foreign Affairs webpage as follows:

"Yom Kippur, eight days after Rosh Hashanah, is the day of atonement, of Divine judgment, and of "affliction of souls'" (Lev. 23:26-32) so that the individual may be cleansed of sins. The only fast day decreed in the Bible, it is a time to enumerate one's misdeeds and contemplate one's faults. The Jew is expected, on this day, to pray for forgiveness for sins between man and God and correct his wrongful actions against his fellow man. The major precepts of Yom Kippur - lengthy devotional services and a 25-hour fast - are observed even by much of the otherwise secular population. The level of public solemnity on Yom Kippur surpasses that of any other festival, including Rosh Hashanah. The country comes to a complete halt for 25 hours on this day; places of entertainment are closed, there are no television and radio broadcasts (not even the news), public transport is suspended, and even the roads are completely closed. Yom Kippur in Israel has special meaning due to memories of the 1973 war, a surprise attack launched by Egypt and Syria against Israel on that very day."

To sum up, Yom Kippur is very important in the Jewish faith, and for a person to turn their back on the holiday maybe spiritual suicide or political suicide as it pertains to that person's acceptance by the church. A baseball player, of Jewish descent, that had to make a decision to reverence Yom Kippur, rather than play baseball was the subject of David Leonard's article "To Play or Pray? Shawn Green and His Choice over Atonement." If a Christian misses Christmas or Easter service, they can catch it on TV or vow to participate next year with no spiritual fallout from the church internally.

These are typically the largest days Christians attend church even if they don't come all year. It would appear people come to keep an invisible Christian card they use when asked, "What's your religion." Some would further explain these two days are better than being a frequent visitor throughout the year.

One thing is for sure, Shawn became the talk of

When and Why Pray

the Jewish church and the public when he announced he wouldn't play and didn't, and likewise, when he said he wouldn't play and did.

"Green was caught in a cultural paradox: playing on Yom Kippur was a betrayal to many in the Jewish community, yet embracing his religion/Jewishness appealed to many fans' American Dream sensibilities. Shawn Green's dilemma is one of accommodation and assimilation: should he heed the call to pray, or the obligation to play? His internal conflict reflects the external intersections of whiteness and Jewishness—American and foreigner—that take place in the realm of sports celebrity culture, and how these relationships inform the meaning, and making, of an American Jewish identity (Leonard 2007:151)."

Leonard points to an interesting undertone of how prayer impacts politics, perhaps how religion in large part does, with the War on Terror related to 9/11 and World War II. "From 1924 to World War II, Jews got more and more "white" within the popular imagination; in the years leading up to the civil rights movement and now through the War on Terror, "whiteness" of American Jews has been accentuated within both popular and political discourses, allowing for greater acceptance, privilege, and performative possibilities of Jewishness. These shifts, especially given the reliance of Jewish identity on being Othered, on being under attack, have resulted in certain levels of ambivalence and uncertainty about what it means to be Jewish in America (Leonard 2007:152)."

Shawn, after 9/11 and hearing a message from Rabbi Simeon Kolko, decided to get more involved with the Jewish community and his inspiration to pray was because of "…so many troubling events and devastating tragedies taking place over the past few weeks, it is important for all of us to come together with love, grief and prayer (Leonard 2007:153)." He skipped playing on Yom Kippur in 2001 and the world celebrated him, Jew and American, but in 2004 the question would be asked again, "Would he play or pray?" Papers, headlines, and articles wrote titles such as, "caught between faith and team, between game and synagogue, and between pennant race and prayers (Leonard 2007:154)."

Green's ultimate decision to play one game and skip the less important game, Rabbi Wolpe turned on Green, and blamed his decision to play instead of praying on his greed for money, "the power of the cash (Leonard 2007:163)." Rabbie Wolpe, comments, that Leonard argue takes a reactionary tone of anxiety and fear, changing from celebration and praise from years prior (Leonard 2007:163). "Is there no room in this society to make a statement that says, 'Money does not override everything? In an age when athletes shift cities the way they change socks, and fans know it is all about money, wouldn't it be great if someone said, in clear, ringing tones, it is actually not about money…teammates expectations…[but] a tradition that is about 3,000 years older than the Dodgers…(Leonard 2007:163)."

Green's celebrity status seemed to be a benefit to the church when he was following tradition, but when he didn't, he became the stumbling block, a sellout and they hated the fame he had acquired. But is the only reason to pray to participate in tradition? Are people's personal relationships with the higher power limited to

When and Why Pray
designated days and times to pray?

The Jew is not the only one that has special times to pray, the Christian has a watch schedule that even the devil worshiper, psychic, or witch is mentioned. The Bible refers to these time slots as "watches". There is Biblical evidence on the watch hours where certain prayers need to be heard or will be answered by God.

For example, Cornelius in Acts 10:1-5 received a vision during the 9th hour, which is the 8th watch. He demonstrates how this timeframe should be set aside for denying oneself and focusing on God. Peter went into a trance in Acts 10:9-15 when he prayed about the 6th hour which is the 7th watch.

This is a time to rest at God's feet and listen. 1st Samuel 11:11, Exodus 14:24, and Lamentations 2:19 also mention different watches. So knowing the watches and what they mean can add value for when to pray. The United Christian Canton website expounds greatly on the subject which will be summarized here for a quick read.

• First Watch: Evening 6:00pm to 9:00pm: A time of quiet reflection or meditation. This time is for declarations and utterances; equipping Christians for service by transforming their minds (Grace 2009). Within the Bible, Jesus healed people in Luke 4:40 and Mark 1:32 during this watch. In addition, Matthew 14:23 also records a time Jesus went aside to pray.

• Second Watch: 9:00pm to 12:00am: Intercessors are at work. Intercessors are at work during this period of time, praying for the cancelation of demonic oppression, plans, and workings. At this time, those gifted with praying abilities can also focus on people who have diseases, heartaches, sickness, torment or are in need of divine interference. Intercessors should pray until their assigned task is completed, released, or resolved.

The aforementioned watches happen before the witching hour. It is believed Satanists along with various idol worshippers (pagans) started casting spells and sending spirits to bring destruction throughout the land at this time. Intercessors are praying to cancel these plans and help people suffering under a satanic yoke.

Between 9pm and 12am this is the best time for decreeing and declaring all negative actions to be changed into positives. Another translation for the importance of this hour is that it is a time for forgiveness, as well as healing physically and in relationships. It is also the time to pray for scientific and technological advances and entries (Grace 2009).

- Third Watch: 12:00am to 3:00am: The witching, warfare, and spiritual direction hours. Believers are not at war with people but rather unclean spirits and demons in high places (Ephesians 6:12). These hours are the times when high spiritual battles take place.

Both sides are praying to command the dawning day and its happenings. This critical time is when captives are set free through warfare in the Spiritual realm. Spiritual warfare is speaking The Word over a circumstance in prayer or declaring it over the situation.

This ideal time is when spiritual strength and direction are best sought after. A testing of the will may also occur like what was true for Peter when he denied knowing Christ (Matthew 26:34, 74). This is a time when the captives can pray for deliverance and receive it. When Apostle Paul and Silas were locked in prison, they prayed during this powerful hour. At this time the jail cell was shaken, opening for their release (Acts 16:25-26).

This time is also ideal to pray for the day and make declarations. This is a critical time for commanding the atmosphere, requesting direction and power according to God's given authority. Demonic energy is also at an all-time high during the witching period. This time frame is when those who practice spells, magic, or dark abilities perform rites.

This is also a time when intercessors feel the need to pray against strongholds so the enemy's plans are disrupted. Christians believe if believers are not praying against Satan's ways, there is no opposition to the devil. There is a spiritual fight and the battle belongs to God, but He uses man through prayer to usher in His will (2 Chronicles 20:15).

- Fourth Watch: 3:00am to 6:00am: Command your morning. This time is for declaring God's Word. In this watch, believers are instructed to command their day. Early in the morning will I seek God's face; making Him a priority reads Psalm 63:1. People waking at 6 a.m. or sooner to pray and seek the Lord's face, are intentional. The Lord expects people when they pray to make preparations for Him because He enjoys Christians who remember His Word; and then, declare that Word over the day and under any circumstance.

- Fifth Watch: 6:00am to 9:00am: Time that God strengthens His children. These hours suit the purpose of the Holy Spirit to prepare man for service. Prayer during this watch should be for equipping the saints to serve God's purpose on that day. Believers need prayer for spiritual strength to be of service throughout the day arguable so do other religions like the Muslim. Christians believe without prayer, God's children won't have the power to make it successfully through the challenges in their day.

- Sixth Watch: 9:00am to 12:00pm: Time to see God's promises fulfilled. Time to reflect on the cross' power. Monotheistic prayers and perhaps more specifically worshipers are not likely going to go 24 hours not reflecting on what God has done and is doing for them. Their prayers, as a form of worship, show their appreciation or gratitude toward God. During this time believers should make an effort to reflect on all God has done for mankind through the cross.

The Jew sets aside time to reflect on the Great Exodus every year, reflecting on what God has done and is doing even up-to-date to keep them safe. It can be said, that redemption is found through remembering all that God has done and making it personal. God delivered the Hebrew nation from Pharaoh after hearing their cries. Some could also say, God delivered the blacks in America in the same way. The Jews were instructed not to forget His promises; but with the promise of the rainbow, Jews and Christians alike could state the world should do the same.

- Seventh Watch: 12:00pm to 3:00pm: Time to reside in the secret place of The Most High. This is a time

When and Why Pray

to sit at the feet of God and listen. Some think prayer is all about talking to God, and forget that people must listen also.

Lyndon Baines Johnson says, "If you're not listening. Then you are not learning." Moltmann quotes Calvin, Francis of Assisi, and Carson in his article "The World is Full of Praise," and he writes:

"The modern world for its part has led to what Rachel Carson called 'the silent spring', and has turned the song of praise of living creation into the stillness of the dead and ravaged world. But the world is not mute. All creatures speak, even if human beings can no longer hear them. All creatures are aflame with the present glory of the Lord, and reflect his glory in a thousand different mirrors, but 'we are blind, we have no eyes' said Calvin, as did Francis of Assisi (99)."

So, it can be understood that effective communication is listening and speaking.

- Eighth Watch: 3:00pm to 6:00pm: Hours of dying to self and rejoicing in the power of Jesus Christ. Rejoicing in Jesus Christ's power means trusting His abilities over natural limitations. Remember all things are possible and anything a believer asks in His name can be granted (John 14:14). Praying during this time acknowledges The Lord's will and man decreases in control so that God may increase (John 3:30). This is the time people are to neglect self and rejoice in God.

There are 8 different documented watches for man to pray. These watches are not set to limit the prayer request of man nor determine the frequency by which people pray. These groups of hours to the contrary provide subject matters for prayer and help man understand what takes place in heaven or in the spiritual realm. "[Prayer]… is talking to God and with God, and if in the fellowship of Christ God is 'our Father,' then his children will like to talk to him, always and everywhere (Moltmann 1997:101)." The Christian believes there are no set times that one must communicate with God, but all these things and more should be prayed as needed, daily.

The Muslims would disagree, as there are set times, to be specific, five times each day they must pray. No matter what is going on in one's life, in the world, in sports, on a job, or in a city, the Muslim is required to pray. If they forget such times, there is a prayer call that is announced to remind all Muslims to pray.

According to the article, Salat: Daily Prayers published by the BBC in 2009, these are the five times a Muslim should pray every day:

- Salat al-fajr: dawn, before sunrise.
- Salat al-zuhr: midday, after the sun passes its highest.
- Salat al-'asr: the late part of the afternoon.
- Salat al-maghrib: just after sunset.
- Salat al-'isha: between sunset and midnight.

Although their time frame is not determined by a clock on the wall, it is set by the setting of the sun. That being the case, the sun sets in different places at different times, so one can argue, a specific time is not set aside. When Muslims make salat, it is believed they are joining themselves with fellow believers, uniting themselves in body, mind, and soul (BBC 2009).

Some years ago, specifically in 2004, there was a political outcry when the al-Islah Islamic Center's leaders petitioned Hamtramck's city council in January 2004 for permission to broadcast the adhan, or call to prayer… (Weiner 2014:1050). "No one openly contested Muslims' right to worship in their mosques, but neighbors resisted and regarded as inappropriate this public pronouncement of Islamic presence that audibly intruded upon public space. Despite constitutional guarantees of free exercise, many suggested that there was a proper time, place, and decibel level for religious practice (Weiner 2014:1050)."

Contrary to thought, the adhan and its broadcasters were not marginalized but affirmed by the City Council that approved their request. Many arguing to support the request, suggested the Catholic bells, operated by the Polish Catholic community, were just as intrusive on public space with the ringing of the bells as the prayer call would be (Weiner 2014:1057). The prayer call was intended to help Muslims remember their home country and bring a little bit of home to Michigan (Weiner 2014:1054).

One thing Abdul Motlib did "[recognize] that other residents might hear the adhan differently. In fact, he did not know how they would respond to it, and he wanted 'to be a good neighbor,' he explained (Weiner 2014:1056)." Although the mosque may have been granted a place with their prayer call, similar to how the church bell rings, their prayer call has become nothing more than ambient noise.

"While there has been periodic squabbling over

its volume, city residents mostly have come to take its presence for granted. Just as Muslims hear the chimes of church bells multiple times a day, Christians also have grown accustomed to being called to pray five times a day by the voice of the muezzin. As with church bells, in other words, it seems that the adhan has gained legitimacy not by making itself heard, but by escaping notice. It has become as normal as the other sounds of religious particularity that regularly spill over onto Hamtramck's supposedly secular streets (Weiner 2014:1072)."

Earlier in the article, it pointed to the idea, that instead of the call meaning Muslims pray, or those that hear it to pray like a Muslim, people hear the call and pray to whatever they believe. So the Christian prays to the Christian God, the Buddhist to their presence, the Catholic, so forth and so forth. What he wanted was to attract people to think the way he does, but, this fusion attempt only alluded to his close desire, to encourage Muslims to come to the mosque to pray.

In understanding when to pray, and why to pray seem to coincide. Understanding the reason for the watches, or the message behind the prayer call, the first answer for why to pray is provided. The follow-up to why pray, is where the prayers were answered or did they go unanswered?

When and Why Pray

TC Martin

Prayer Still Works

How can anybody argue that prayer works if there are those who claim to have prayed, and their prayers go unanswered? To understand the statement, "I prayed and my prayers went unanswered," again the conversation has to be revisited as to what connotes unanswered prayer. If prayer is simply asking, or making a petition, an entreaty to God to do this or that, perhaps there is room for unanswered prayer.

But what if another idea is valid, in that prayer is not just a moment to bark orders at God, but to have a two-way conversation similar to what Moses had with God? Is it possible to have an answer and simply not like the response? A big miss, in many of the articles I have studied, is the free will of God. Shane Sharp, wrote about the reason his subjects believed their prayers went unanswered in his article, When Prayers Go Unanswered.

His study was on women in abusive relationships and their desire to pray their way or the ability to accept where they are. This article misses the Character of God, in that, it would never be God's will for a woman, or man, for that matter to be physically abused. Nowhere in scripture, Christians can argue, does it grant permission for men to beat women. The Bible instead, says for men to love their wives and for women to respect their husbands (Ephesians 5:33).

So the reason women end up in brutal relationships is not God's will, nor His character, but a choice of the person. Many of these women, who prayed during these relationships, reported to Sharp, their prayers went unanswered because God didn't change the abuser. In relation to this article, a question, is God supposed to fix people He did not link a person with? Scripture says, "Do not be unequally yoked if a believer is married to an unbeliever they are only to stay with them if they don't hinder God's plan for the believers' life (1 Corinthians 7:14-17)."

If a person is being abused, or kept from the truths God presents about them, how is staying with the abuser in right standing of God? The article speaks not of this reality but of the reality of free will for men. It writes that the prayers of these women are being justified on God-serving justification so as to not disrupt their religious beliefs and yet maintain their position.

A studied Christian would have the ability to stand on scripture that says, God can save a person and their whole house, as is recorded in 1 Corinthians 7. It speaks about the unsaved being covered by the saved spouse's prayers. So, yes, one person can pray for another, but if one wants to leave, hence, not stay and be covered under the prayer the Bible says to let them go. Marianne, a woman involved in the study, "The suffering at the hands of others is the price humans just pay, so to speak, to have free will ("But if we're gonna have free choice, then we're stuck with, with all the negatives and the maniacs on the planet, too") (Sharp 2013:8)." Some women allude to them being in this situation to learn a lesson, which to some people can be understood as cruel.

The question must be asked, does one not know, that for every action there is a reaction? If a person makes a choice, that choice impacts others around them. God says to take everything to Him in prayer (Philippians 4:6).

If taken at His word, that would imply a person asked a question and waited for the answer. How can anyone assume that a person did that, or ignore if they didn't, and then hold the accusation that God doesn't answer prayers over His power? The Bible makes it no secret that God makes the choice to have mercy on whom He chooses, and to yield His sovereign right over humanity how He determines.

Buddhists, rationalists, and atheists understand this power as tyranny, but is that not what they do in their own thoughts? Are they not playing god to themselves if they pray and seek some positive change coming from their inner self projected out? Christians would have this gripe against this group, "Is it okay for you to subject others to your thoughts and conclusions, but God, the creator of all living, cannot make choices that you disagree with?"

Prayer Still Works

Unlike a pagan god, or idol, that is shaped out of stone or wood, and can fit in the palm of a person's hand, God is a living breathing Spirit (John 4:24). His thoughts and ways are above mans, what is impossible for terrestrial creatures, God can do by celestial means (Luke 18:27). Likewise, if a person prays certain times a day, performs rituals in a temple, it means nothing if it doesn't impact the person the acts are performed for. Jesus said, the things the Jews did were to bless God, but their hearts were not in the right place so they became nothing more than a tradition of men.

It would appear that prayer works, it just may not pan out in the way a person thinks it should. Many of the ladies caught in the abusive situations, used their prayer life to help build their self-worth of confidence to leave, and helped them endure if they chose to stay. They pointed to scripture to remind them when they were being torn down verbally by their spouse, what God said about them. Thinking on scripture and praying the Word, is what they said pulled them out of the situation and kept a bad situation from getting worse.

Not only did these women attest to God and prayer working aside from the person they prayed for changing, they realized the answer to their prayer was locked in not answering another. Their freedom to live the life God intended for them, had to happen out of the reach of their previous relationship. The man they thought was to remain their husband, was not a part of God's plan.

I argue the man was never part of the plan. Marianne mentioned living in a free world with the maniacs comes with the territory. What if she is among the number of maniacs? At some point, a person should ask the question, "Am I hurting myself to make this choice? Are my choices hurting my body, mind, or spirit? Who needs the maniac of the world to be a threat, when the one inside is the bigger and real threat?"

A big prayer request many intercessors pray about daily is breaking generational curses and soul ties. If a person desires God to answer their prayers, they have to be willing to ask the question, wait for the response, and follow the instructions. Ms. Yulanda, a woman who was in an abusive relationship, married a guy she knew was not the man promised some years ago to her in a prophecy. The man she married was aggressive, opinionated, controlling, and not a believer.

She married him anyway and throughout the dating experience, she was not unaware of his attitude, temper, or violent behaviors. "She knew he wasn't saved and had no interest in being saved, but she thought she could change him." The relationship ended the same way it began, with her knowing he was wrong for her the entire time. Her unanswered prayer was the catalyst for her ministry.

When some of us get a "no" from God it is to help direct our next step, likewise when we receive a "yes." One thing Ms. Yulanda had to say, "Make no mistake about it, I ask for a lot of things in prayer, just because I don't get what I ask for, doesn't mean my prayer is unanswered. Sometimes I get a 'no,' 'not yet,' 'or give me time.' I am the one that has to understand His answer and accept it."

Leo Tolstoy said, "Everyone thinks of changing

the world, but no one thinks of changing himself." If this statement is true, then people simply refuse to do the work for self-fulfillment. Agreeing with Oprah Winfrey, "We can't become what we need to be by remaining what we are." Imagine, an all-you-can-eat buffet; everyone has the ability to pray and to whom they choose. Although the options are before them, they must make a plate and eat.

Just like Daniel who chose God's diet over his enemies, who ate choice meat (Daniel 1:15) and prayed 3 times per day. He believed his prayer life and diet were superior to the king's diet, and after a time, they looked at Daniel and compared his health to the others who followed the king's diet. The findings, like today, prayer helps reduce pain in patience, gives confidence for new life or for healing to take place, and brings peace no matter the outcome.

A few stories must be shared about people who got the victory after going through their God experiences. A woman many R&B fans are familiar with who has an amazing testament to long-term prayer is Angie Stone. Angie is a modern-day singer known for her popular tunes that encourage people of color. Both men and women can listen to her music for encouragement. She did not quickly rise in grandeur even though gifted as a vocalist, writer, and producer; her heart was set on helping people.

Angie seemed to have risen very quickly in fame but her journey took over 20 years in development. How many would have quit or attributed the delay to unanswered prayer? If one quits seeking the answer, can that be called unanswered prayer on God's part? Angie

Stone had much faith and hope in The Lord for which He rewarded her handsomely she believes and others would agree.

Jesus prayed about a dreadful cup He must drink, asking for it to be removed from Him. Nevertheless, Jesus' desire was for His father "…not my will, but thine, be done" (Luke 22:42). If Jesus changed his mind, that would have drastically changed the redemption story. All decisions individuals make in response to their prayers or otherwise, would appear to impact others.

So, is it possible to pray and ask God for requests that may not be granted and He still loves you? Sure, it is possible—and yes He still loves the believer! He loved His son the Christians believe, and yet, He didn't change the cup he had to drink.

The veil would not have been torn. Keys to hell, death, and the grave would still be in possession of Satan if Jesus did not drink his cup. Remember, "All things work together for good to them that love God… (Romans 8:28)." Another well-known celebrity known for His belief in God and prayer is Tony Dungy.

For several years, Tony was a head coach for the Indiana Colts football team. He worked hard and was one of the few black or minority coaches in the league. He was a faithful, devout believer in front and behind the cameras. Many liked and followed his career because of the character he displayed and like Sean Green, he was a beacon to his community both black and Christian.

Tony worked hard and also prayed to win a Super Bowl ring. The prayer was answered in his last year before he retired, but some may say look how long it took. A follow-up question, did Tony appreciate it more because he had to work and wait for it?

Sometimes prayers are not only for the person's benefit but also for those around them. Whenever disasters happen in life, the biggest request one would likely hear is for prayers (Ephesians 6:18-19). Job, a mighty man in the Bible, was commanded by God to pray concerning his friend's safety and not just for himself. His friends accused him of being the problem, while God was using Job to pray for mercy aimed at them. People may not always know the reasons behind The Lord's decision, but their hearts should be set on God. Prayer is an act of obedience, which causes God to incline His ear towards request.

Another account that must be shared to encourage anyone debating whether prayer still works is Apostle James Duncan. He is a native of Guyana, an international business consultant, conference speaker, counselor, senior pastor, also one founding apostle for Christ Church International and Global Harvest Apostolic Prophetic Network. His partner is a prophetess and his wife is Donna Duncan. He has raised up apostles and prophets within Africa, the Caribbean, the US, and across Europe. He also created the Christ Prophetic Academy Worldwide, with headquarters located in Brooklyn, New York.

He looked like many before accepting his call into ministry. Life was happening; he had a family with children and was serving the Lord with his gifts. He too was not immune to the rain falling on him, as the

Bible promises; "[God] sendeth rain on the just and on the unjust" (Matt. 5:45). An ear infection disrupted the nerves in his face causing it to collapse. At a visit to his doctor in 1989, Apostle Duncan was diagnosed with Bell's Palsy. The prognosis was, "There is no cure."

Doctors said he would be forever paralyzed, living with a distortion of the face, and damaged vision, and speech. Throughout this diagnosis, he heard the Lord whisper in his ear, "I am the same yesterday, today, and forever." So he concluded in a personal interview that if "He healed others in the past and is still healing, He could heal me too," he said.

In his interview, Apostle Duncan was asked why he believed the promise that God whispered. He said, "Isaiah 53:5 says, by His stripes you are healed. If man says there is no cure for my ailment, let God be true and let every man be a liar. I chose to believe in God. That is why I am healed." He also believed in the voices of more than one prophet from different regions who spoke to him. Confirming God's words that say, "In the mouth of two or three witnesses shall every word be established (2 Corinthians 13:1)."

The first step that Apostle Duncan took in achieving his miracle was to go on a 3 day fast. Once the Lord gave direction, between 6 and 7 months straight Apostle was faithful to His voice. Within a year time, the impossible was made possible. He no longer had to wear dark glasses or hats going outside, but was totally restored, no extra protection needed!

He was not discouraged from waiting faithfully for his miracle. It did not come overnight, but the Lord is faithful, and he was patiently waiting on God to do His perfect work—yes even in the face of daily facts that spoke contrary. He also used biblical stories such as Job's, to encourage him on his journey. He said, "Everyone has to stay encouraged and steadfast with the truth that God cares about all situations. Then, stand firm in The Lord's words of promise."

A truth that must be told according to Apostle Duncan, "Being encouraged and trusting God, triggered His power to operate." "I focused and meditated on what The Lord said about His promises coming to pass because God's Word cannot return unto Him void (Isaiah 55:11)." Advice that Apostle Duncan desired to share in his interview also includes:

"Put your full confidence in the Lord and trust what he has prophesied to you. Job had the same views when he said, "Though he slay me, yet will I trust in him (Job 13:15). Miracles are instantaneous; just remember healing is a process."

An administrator in education testified about her God encounter, first with a few questions. The interviewee said in a series of questions and answers that she prays daily and sometimes prays "long and hard" for results. She participated in "shut-ins" and was active in church.

She did what she knew pleased God, but also made mistakes that displeased Him. She said, "Have you been hit by a storm so strong it left you terrified that you resorted to earthly resolve? So have I. This is my story of how God drew me into Him, by showing me that yes I pray, but my minuscule faith was unable to support my earthly resolve in my time of need."

She continued, "But God, thank you for being faithful according to Psalm 138: 1-3 in the Message. Also thank you for keeping me, in spite of my double-minded behavior– James 1:5-8. The passage reads in the Message Bible:

"If you don't know what you're doing, pray to the Father. He loves to help. You'll get his help, and won't be condescended to when you ask for it. Ask boldly, believingly, without a second thought. People who "worry their prayers" are like wind-whipped waves. Don't think you're going to get anything from the Master that way, adrift at sea, keeping all your options open."

Answered prayers build strength, belief, and faith in general and it would appear in prayers being answered.

Her son, whom she always prayed would never have negative interactions with the law, was arrested not once, but twice in three months. This young man got into trouble at twenty years old, twice, in two different states. In both state's jurisdictions, it is understood the District Attorneys are tough and jail time is the only option for the charges he was facing.

She said her world fell apart; she began to see doom and despair for a long moment but knew this mother had to fight that feeling. This woman began researching and calling every justice program she knew to see what they could do. She distinctly remembers crying, but also wailing for hours, days, and weeks. Not seeing a way out, all avenues explored were costly and did not guarantee an escape from this nightmare. Exhausting all her earthly know-how, and still feeling lost and afraid, she finally called on her God. He was always there, but the gripping fear had her so that she could not experience His ever-present help in her time of need before now (Psalm 46:1).

God showed up by guiding her to a first-time offender's program. This program was designed to give a person's getting into trouble for the first time a second chance. This chance allowed them to correct their wrong, and not have a criminal record attached to their name. "Glory to God!" she loudly exclaimed, being oh so happy. Despite her fear and doubt, God came through. She stated, "Having this victory in hand, I felt ashamed that I did not trust God." "He loves me so much that He wants good and not evil for me and my family (Jeremiah 29:11)."

She continued her dialogue with: "There I was rejoicing and thanking God for granting us His favor with man. Little did I know the second test was right behind the first." One Sunday morning, a month later, the phone rang; it was an unexpected call from jail in another state. Shocked, hoping she heard wrong, while her stomach churned, this mother wished it to be a wrong number, but deep down inside she knew the call was correct. The call was dropped before anyone could speak and the connection was lost. She hoped it was the wrong number. It was Sunday, The Lord's Day, supposed to be good.

"No, no, no," she said aloud, "This can't be for real. God just blessed us with favor. If this phone call is true, the current program he just got into is out the window for sure, and he will go to jail. Oh! God, this is not happening" she replied. Moments later, the phone rang again and yes it was for her. Her son was calling from jail in another state. "This can't be for real; it must be a nightmare, a dream. I pray I tithe, I love God, this is not supposed to happen. Oh God, help me, what do I do?" She called her sister in Christ for support and advice on what to do next.

An extra factor to his troubles was that he was caught in possession of a loaded gun, having 6 bullets. The mandatory prison sentence for such an offense is 3.5 years in jail and three years probation. The case within another state required him to serve 1-3 years in prison, per offense. He was accused of 11 offenses, and there were threats to add 4 additional charges making it a total of 15. Both cases dragged on for over a year. She watched God touch the judge's heart in his first case; which he repeatedly pushed back waiting for a verdict in the second incident to determine if he would proceed with prosecution.

As the cases dragged on, her faith in The Lord increased to believe what God said all along. She declared, "God strengthened my faith by teaching me how to stand in Your word, to believe that you can do all things through as Ephesians 3:20-21." God revealed to her and promised, "He is in control. No trial. No jail time. No record. Each time we went to court, no matter what was said, I stood on God's promise to me". When a person gets prophetic advice they must stand on it. She said, "There were times I felt afraid; there were times the verdict appeared to be final and against what God said. But I recited what God said, despite what was playing out in the courtroom before me."

She was pleased to say; "One case was dismissed,

Prayer Still Works

No trial, No jail time. I believe in God for the final part of His promise, of No Record. In the second case, despite many attempts to deny his entrance back into The First Time Offenders program, he was accepted and has successfully completed it with resounding praise. God is faithful, just, and true to His word.

God cannot lie, if He promises a thing, He is faithful to perform it (Numbers 23:19). Her confidence in God and His Word is greater because of this experience". Finally, she declared, "Though it happened to my son, it was for me, too. Romans 8:28, "And we know that all things work together for good to them that love God, to them who are the called according to his purpose." "This pain was great, the spiritual reward and growth were greater, glory to my Father God in heaven for His grace and mercy. Halleluiah!"

A retired captain from the New York City correction department, Joel Parker experienced an early warning of catastrophe getting ready to take place through divine hearing. Unaware of timing and not understanding the overwhelming noise was compelling enough to act within his personal jurisdiction. Just at the end of a 9 intense hour work schedule, there was "radio silence."

This form of action caused all communication going and coming from outside his work site to be stopped unless it was ordered through the prison warden. Oblivious to the calamity that stunned New Yorkers, about 45 minutes after Mr. Parker's premonition, an American Airlines flight # 11 plane hit the north tower of The World Trade Center. 18 min later United Airlines flight # 175 hit the south tower.

These actions were the beginning of air traffic attacks on U.S. soil becoming known as 911 orchestrated by terrorists. Mr. Parker's spiritual insight, the visions he was seeing, and the noise he heard ringing in his ear, prompted an early lockdown. Confused, he did not know if the noise and visions were real or simply " pre-amplified visions."

When his chief showed up with a team, surprised they found out this was the only site secured on Rikers Island. It was hard to explain the reason for calling a shutdown to his boss. The person he would have gotten permission to do such actions during a disastrous time.

He asked his superiors to turn on their televisions, but they were unable to receive any reception. The Lord directed him to have them turn on their radios; so that is what he told his superiors. When getting directions from God, He leads people to perfect peace and is willing to follow Him and listen.

They were then able to hear that an aircraft hit a building in the city of New York. Hearing natural airway confirmation, Mr. Parker was in crisis mode, which he began preparing from his spiritual insight downloaded earlier. Receiving the appropriate call going into "red alert" was given. Having experienced crises in the past he was ready.

Prior to this happening, the administration was dealing with him hard. Giving him an overwhelming amount of paperwork, and adding various positions into his already intense work duties. This added pressure caused him to seek God more to strengthen him spiritually in withstanding the negative attacks he was under. He was motivated to have consistent prayer and Bible reading time, which caused him to become more sensitive towards God. Management that was tough on him turned to his level of experience in handling this rare matter.

He worked another shift due to the lack of workers. Unable to determine the prisoner's reaction to the current news, he provided assurance for inmates. Help to soothe the composure of prisoners and staff with his comforting words from God performing as a chaplain of sorts. His divine connection allowed him to fulfill a duty he never openly performed before.

He was led by God as an oracle to the people in his circle. Being in a place to fulfill the prophetic utterance of foretelling. The man of God gave exhortation, edification, and comfort to individuals for this current situation. He performed his job above and beyond expectations. When he left the job, it took more than 4 people to replace him.

Prophet Andre Cook, from a local church in Queens, spoke a word from the Lord to his congregation, "An unspeakable tragedy would happen that could not be avoided. Everyone was told to change the way they traveled going and coming from their home and work. The Lord's people were warned to change their daily routines."

He said, "Whatever form of transportation used to go to and from work, or home, you must change." "Those who take a bus, change to train. Those who walk, take a cab. If you go home walking on the left side of the street, change to the right side."

The congregation was directed to start changing our routes beginning that day with an unknown end date. People's reactions were stunned due to the fact many individuals only knew one way. On 9/11 everyone who was under this prophetic umbrella that worked near or in the towers did something different.

People, who were usually early to work, ended up late because they did something different. One decided to eat breakfast from a food truck, which they never did before. Some happened to call out from work that day, and as a result, were saved.

A mighty woman of God, Vernistine "Glo" Dove, who resides in the smallest state in America, Rhode Island, skillfully demonstrated God's BIG power to a small problem for Him, through prayer. She had no idea of an incomprehensible storm, set to hit her life, moments after a normal Sunday morning service. A celebrated day in Christendom faith, Pentecostal Sunday, was also her beloved husband of 42 years, birthday that year.

He just finished delivering an encouraging, uplifting sermon to his churchgoers. Bishop Dwight made an unusual, but sensible request, to his son for a glass of ice-cold water, walking towards the office. While in the room sitting and talking to staff, within minutes he became confused asking, "What is this I have in my hand?" which was his cell phone.

Then Bishop's head became lethargic, falling

backward along with the eyes, giving no response to his name being called. A staff member then hurried to get his wife. She rushed in having no time to think, and called her emergency contact, God. Moments later, her 3rd son Bruce announced, "Ma he's gone, you might as well forget it, go and call the ambulance."

She refused to acknowledge such a decree and did what she knew, prayed. She immediately trusted in her faith, standing on Matthew 17:20 "…if you have faith as a mustard seed, you will say to this mountain, 'Move from here to there,' and it will move, and nothing will be impossible for you."

The news was grim, her beloved husband and faithful servant of God was dead, according to reports from the hospital. Proof was the coagulated blood which was a thick black mass drawn from his veins. Faced with these daunting facts, her faith in The Creator, and Jesus Christ, had to be greater than the reality she was seeing. She did not become saddened or allow bad news to cause depressed emotions to form actions but renounced obvious proof for the true facts of God.

Bishop Dwight P. Dove, Presiding Prelate of Morning Star Fellowship Assemblies, is an earthly vessel carrying the great "I AM, THAT I AM" (Exodus 3:14). Therefore Jesus's life must manifest in his body. She believed and spoke those things that did not exist as though they did. Her level of faith caused a manifestation to be seen. Her "honey" was still alive. She stood confidently saying, "When storms hit your life, turn to Jesus, like the disciples in Mark 4:36-38."

Today, the way her husband jumps and skips

energetically shows no evidence that he ever died or is even a senior citizen. When there is an encounter with God, it changes a person. What a person believes does impact the results of their prayers. One must believe that God is able and willing to accomplish what "He sets out to do (Isaiah 55:11)."

There is no easy process for receiving an answered prayer. No one knows a special system to get it faster, consistently, or otherwise. One must remember the Word about God's character and expectation for prayer. God gives man the way, but they have a choice to take it.

A Personal Testimony

My life is truly a testament to God's goodness and faithfulness. I remember some key moments in my personal story where I was forced to call on the name of the Lord because no other reputable person would do. A personal lesson was having faith in God to help me trust people.

Being an American-born child, having a father from Cuba and a mother Jamaican was normal until I was mixed with other kids who did not. What I thought was standard was seen as a threat. Unaware of my parents being envisioned as intruders became a hard fact to contend with. Many Americans during my developmental stages were propagandized to hate the influx of foreigners.

It was hard growing up proud to be yourself, but nervous that your friends would disown you if they knew my immediate family ancestry. It was a challenge to fit in among those whom I grew up with when they didn't come from another country. The social norms of Brooklyn surely weren't the Islands or vice versa. I had to pray many of nights for the right way to be me and not offend anyone. Of course, bending too much to please others, meant I then had to start praying for who I was, became, and was born to become.

Knowing I am not the only one who struggled to find identity my plans are on writing about this journey. Another major challenge was being diagnosed with a debilitating disease with no cure at this time, diagnosed as MS. I wanted to ask so many people, "Why me," "Why now?" I quickly realized people cannot always answer these tough questions, but God can. No matter how smart the doctors were, or how sensitive, they kept me holding on like a Band-Aid to an open wound with their updates of no change.

It showed me my trust and faith was in the wrong place. It was in my doctor's abilities and not The Great Physician (John 5:1-9). Prayer changes things because having a conversation invites The Lord into your problem for Him to bring about resolve. A scar may be left to remind you of what happened, but always remember that God resolved it for your healing.

Living with MS was not easy for me to accept and some days I still fight a battle. Currently, my body has lost some mobility but I'm trusting The Lord as I have learned on many occasions. Some of the things that anyone could easily take for granted the Lord is showing me through people I love—and just met how to live this life. If a person knows someone battling an illness, or condition, do know that the Lord is able to

A Personal Testimony

stabilize that person's life despite their instability for an instantaneous miracle. In my case, unanswered prayer was me getting a different answer than I asked for; but I got the answer.

Prayed like Paul to be healed, like I am sure you or they have too, but like him, one is living with a thorn. There is a mighty testimony I must share about God's goodness! Yes, it is a lot more to share, so I plan to publish it in the next book. I must say, before pausing the story, "Everything The Lord does is Perfect." I read that in a chain email forwarded to me by my cousin, and the statement resonated with my reality.

I have learned, that answered prayer may not always be what we want to hear, but it is what is best for us. Because our minds are finite, we don't always see beyond our current circumstances—but God does! It is my intention to write about both these experiences where prayer was my greatest comfort.

Until the next chapter…shalom.

Dr. TC Martin

Conclusion

There has been a lot of data generated on prayer to get estimates on who prays, how many people, and why. Prayer differs from asking, wishing, and hoping, to communicating with God, and performing rites. Although the reason people pray or perform ceremonies differs from worship to tradition, or gaining control over a spirit or oneself, prayer appears to work. Blacks in America perhaps pray the most, because many would argue prayer broke the chains of slavery over their ancestors. The same religion that was used to oppress them, books were removed from their bibles and they weren't accepted into white churches at the onset of conversion, amazingly so, they created their own fellowships that functioned as the heartbeat of the community and helped deliver them from their oppressors.

From Hollywood pictures like Sleepy Hollow where a lady takes the head of a restless horseman stuck in between the throws of one realm and another, she controls the spirit, by the use of a dagger and summoning it. The horror industry keeps pagan traditions alive

Conclusion
by continuing to make movies that glorify dark arts, magic, and sorcery. Another danger that appears to be constant and dire is health issues. Everyone is born to die, no matter how well a person lives, eats, or prays, death is bound to come.

It is at this time a chaplain is longed for. A chaplain is a woman or man of God who prays with their influence to God but doesn't push their faith on another but ushers them if interested into a relationship with God (CICA 2016:18). In the article "Pay as You Pray?," by BMJ, British Medical Journal, they spoke about the lost and dying need of Chaplains. Most hospitals have Chaplains on payroll, but some may argue the need to have a chaplain on payroll may be too much, and perhaps not fit into their professional landscape. BMJ writes:

"Church representatives are afraid that hospital chaplain services will not fit comfortably within the harshly businesslike future about to be ushered in by the reforms. The value of a chaplain's work, they point out, cannot be quantified in purely material terms. The cutting-edge competition, they fear, could prompt some hospitals to opt out of funding chaplaincy services altogether (BMJ 2019)."
"…The chaplain would be privatized, contracting out his spiritual succor to those hospital divisions that might need him, or even, perish the thought, inviting patients to 'pay as you pray (BMJ 2019)."

Although the business world, governments, and people try to shake loose people's foundation in hope, and the belief in the power of prayer, most people still run to the rugged cross in times of need. For Every

Prayer That Goes Unanswered, the article written by Greg Morse, a staff writer with Desiring God, says unanswered prayers shouldn't be taken personally and he emphasizes the good nature of God to answer His people by giving them "good things" when they ask (Morse 2018). He assures that believers will not pray much longer and reassures that for every prayer a Christian prays God hears and will answer no matter the time it takes to fulfill; that is even unto death.

Today the Jew believes he is living in the promise to Abraham. The Blacks believe they are living in the prayers answered by their late and more recent public figures and ancestors. The list can go on and on, some prayers simply take longer than man has days.

What is sure, prayer takes dedication and commitment. Like learning music, anyone can have an opinion on something they hear, but it takes someone studied to offer a valuable critique (Anderson 1931:595). In performing my research reading article after article, and reviewing data, charts, and stories, it is my conclusion prayer works.

With understanding how prayer works, I must also point out that prayer is not the only solution some take to achieve their goals. It is not foreign to read about how some Christians go to psychics, how believers in Rural South Africa profess to be Christian but they will still go and visit sangomas (similar to a witch doctor) at night (King 2012:1177). Life has a way of testing everyone's faith, the same visiting the sangoma only goes for cures for their body, but don't put any trust in the same spirit for their salvation.

Conclusion

Some believe a person can switch the deity or being they pray to and not disrupt their inner core beliefs. It would appear to me that more research should be conducted on how a person reasons that believing and confessing a religion but yet denying the full power it claims, is not a conflict in their ability to follow that religion; or that does not impact their prayer life and relationship with their god/God in any way.

About The Author

Dr. TC Martin is a first-generation Brooklyn baby of Cuban and Jamaican parentage. She is a graduate of the New York City public school system, who was committed to furthering her education. She earned her 1st degree at Borough of Manhattan Community College and continued her education with a Bachelor of Science from Nyack College. Advancing her studies for a Masters from Fordham University and her Doctorate degree from CICA International University and Seminary.

Ministry created opportunities and filled numerous areas of interest for her. She has always been patient about seeing people succeed and live wholesome lives so she merged her love for community with ministry. Obtaining her Ambassador-At-Large Appointment and ordained chaplain license from Word of Life Ministries International, a Non-Governmental Organization (NGO) in Special Consultative Status with the Economic and Social Council of the United Nations (ECOSOC). She pursued her General Practice Psychotherapy

About the Author

(G.P.P.) Under Letters Patent from the Canadian Christian Clinical Counselors Association, Calgary Canada.

Dr. TC currently invests a great deal of her time helping people within different communities. To date, she serves as Bursar, Registrar, and is an assistant teacher for the Prophetic Academy in Brooklyn, N.Y., and TC Safety Agency for Defensive Drivers in NYC, along with assisting various Christian organizations offering administrative and financial advice. She is heavily goal-orientated and fully set on publishing more books and using all the gifts and talents God gave her.

Her future books include working titles, "Bend Don't Break" and "Invisible Storms." She is an advocate for those seeking specific miracles—even the gift of living with reality if the supernatural doesn't appear as believed.

KLEPub.com Store

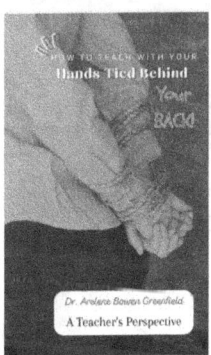

It's time to start and finish **YOUR Story!**

KLF Publishing specializes in helping people become authors. In as little as 15 to 90 days, we can help you develop your book and publish to 39,000 outlets!

Ghostwrite, Edit, Format, Publish
We can help from
Start to Finish.

Bibliography

"Adhan or the Muslim Call to Prayer," AlIslam.org, http://www.alislam.org/book/slalat/adhan-or-muslim-call-to-prayer (Accessed November 30, 2019)

"Our History," AME-Church.com, http://www.ame-church.com/our-church/our-history (Accessed November 30, 2019).

Anderson, W.R. 1931."We Pray for Discipline," The Musical Times, 72:595-596.

Bade, Mary K., Stephen W. Cook. 2008. "Functions of Christian Prayer in the Coping Process," Journal for the Scientific Study of Religion, 47:123-133

Baker, Joseph O. 2008. "An Investigation of the Sociological Patterns of Prayer Frequency and Content," Sociology of Religion, 69:169-185

BBC "Salat: Daily Prayers," BBC, bbc.org, September 8, 2009 https://www.bbc.co.uk/religion/religions/islam/practices/salat.shtml (Accessed December 1, 2019)

BMJ. 1990. "Pay as You Pray?" BMJ: British Medical

Journal 300:630

Brummel, Elizabeth J. 2014. "You Don't Have to Pray to Somebody in Special English': Style, Narration, and Salvation in Urban Kenya. Journal of Religion in Africa 44:251-281

"The Chaplain's Ministry Guide," CICA-International (Canadian International Chaplaincy Association) http://www.cica-international.org (Assessed November 19, 2019)

Catholic News Herald. 2017. "Why Do We Pray for the Dead?" Catholic News Hearld. https://catholicnews-herald.com/faith/funeral/204-news/grief-header/1577-why-do-we-pray-for-the-dead (Accessed November 30, 2019).

Christianity.com "What is Calvinism," Christanity.com. https://www.christianity.com/church/denominations/what-is-calvanism.html (Accessed November 1, 2019).

Cohen, Cynthia B., Sondra E. Wheeler, David A. Scott, Barbara Springer Edwards, Patricia Lusk, and the Anglican Working Group in Bioethics. 2000. "Prayer as Therapy. A Challenge to Both Religious Belief and Professional Ethics." Hastings Center Report. May-June:40-47

Diamant, Jeff. Besheer Mohamed. 2018. "Black Millennials are More Religious Than Other Millennials." Pew Research Center. https://www.pewresearch.org/fact-tank/2018/07/20/black-millennials-are-more-religious-than-other-millennials/ (Accessed November 30, 2019).

EAEC.org. "Roman Catholicism: Founder: Emperor Constantine," EAEC.org. https://www.eaec.org/cults/romancatholic.htm (Accessed December 1, 2019)

Finkelman, Eliezer. 2016-2017. "A Meditation on Petitionary Prayer and Natural Yearning." The Torah U-Madda Journal 17:123-149

Gomez, Brad T., Thomas G. Hansford., George A. Krause. 2007. "The Republicans Should Pray for Rain: Weather, Turnout, and Voting in U.S. Presidential Elections." The Journal of Politics 69:649-663.
Gotthold, Zev. 1961. "Prayer." Tradition: A Journal of Orthodox Jewish Thought. 4:107-123.

Gowler, David B. 2018. "Today Is A National Day of Prayer. Should That Be Legal?" The Washington Post. https://www.washingtongpost.com/news/made-by-history/wp/201//05/03/today-is-a-national-day-of-prayer-should-that-be-legal/?noredirect=on (Accessed August 29, 2019).

Grace, C.B. "Prayer Watches," Ezekiel Regiment Prayer Ministry of San Marcos Texas, March 24, 2009. http://ezekielregiment.wordpress.com/2009/03/24/prayer-watches/ (Accessed March 15, 2019).

Gross, Rita M. 2002. "Meditation and Prayer: A Comparative Inquiry," Buddhist-Christian Studies 22:77-86

Grossman, Cathy Lynn.2015. "Sunday Is Still the Most Segregated Day off the Week," American Magazine. https://www.americanmagazine.org/content/all-things/sunday-still-most-segregated-day-week (Accessed November 30, 2019).

Huda. 2019. "Prayer," Learning Religions.com https://www.learnreligions.com/qiblah-direction-of-makkah-for-prayer-2004517 (Accessed December 1, 2019).

Hawkins, Sean. 1997. "To Pray or Not to Pray: Politics, Medicine, and Conversion among the LoDagaa of Northern Ghana," Canadian Journal of African Studies/Revuew Canadienne Des Etudes Africacines. 31:50-85.

James, Liz. 1996. "Pray Not to Fall into Temptation and Be on Your Guard": Pagan Statues in Christian Constantinople," Gesta 35:12-20.

King, Brian. 2012. "We Pray at the Church in the Day and Visit the Sangomas at Night": Health Discourses and traditional medicine in Rural South Africa. Annals of the Association of American Geographers 102:1173-1181.

Knohl, Israel. 1996. "Between Voice and Silence: The Relationship between Prayer and Temple Cult," Journal of Bilical Literature 115:17-30.

Kurapati, Rajeev MD. 2013. "Why I Pray for My Patients," KevinMD.com https://www.kevinmd.com/blog/2013/08/pray-patients.html (Accessed July 28, 2019)

Leonard, David J. 2007. "To Play or Pray? Shawn Green and His Choice Over Atonement," Shofar, 25:150-167.

Masci, David. 2018. "5 Facts About the Religious Lives of African Americans," Pew Research Center. https://www.pewresearch.org/fact-tank/2018/02/07/5-facts-about-the-religious-lives-of-african-americans/ (Accessed November 30, 2019).

Moltmann, Jugen. 1997. "What are We Doing When We Pray?" From the Source of Life: The Holy Spirit and Theology of Life p. 92-107.

Morse, Greg. 2018. "For Every Prayer that Goes Unanswered," DesiringGod.org. https://www.desiringgod.org/articles/for-every-prayer-that-goes-unanswered (Accessed July 28th, 2019).

Nkomazana, Fidelis. 2015. "Missionary Colonial Mentality and the Expansion of Christianity in Bechuanaland Protectorate, 1800 to 1900," Association of Study of Religion in Southern Africa held at the University of Johannesburg 26-28 October 29-54.

Samuelson, Norbert M. 1993. "The Concept of /Worship in Judaism, In A People Apart: Chosenness and Ritual in Jewish Philosophical Thought, ed. Daniel Frank. 245-261
Schapera, I. 1961. "Livingstone's Missionary Correspondence, 1841 – 1856," Los Angeles: University of California Press. pp. 252

Shapiro, Fred. 2014. "I Was Wrong About the Origin of The Serenity Prayer," HuffPost.com https://www.huffpost.com/entry/serenity-rauer-origin-_n_5331924 (Accessed December 1, 2019).

Sharp, Shane. 2010. "How Does Prayer Help Manage Emotions?" Social Psychology Quarterly 73:417-437

Sharp, Shane. 2013. "When Prayers Go Unanswered,"

Stewart, Malachi. 2011. "The Eight Prayer Watches," Prophetic Streams Ministries. http://www.propheticstreams.webs.com/apps/blog/entries/show/7685793-the-eight-prayer-watches (Accessed September 3, 2012).

The Catholic Layman. 1852. "To Whom Should We Pray?" The Catholic Layman 1:64

United Christian Canton. "Understanding the Eight Prayer Watches," United Christian Canton, UnitedChristianUnion.org, https://united-inchristcanton.org/prayer-resources/understanding-the-eight-prayer-watches-2/ (Accessed March 15, 2019).

Weiner, Isaac A. 2014. "Calling Everyone to Pray: Pluralism, Secularism, and the Adhan in Hamtramck, Michigan," Anthropological Quarterly, 87:1049-1077.

Wikepedia. http://en/m/wikipedia.org/wiki/idolatry (Accessed December 1, 2019).

Willoughby, W.C. 1969. "The Soul of The Bantu." London: London: SCM.

www.ingramcontent.com/pod-product-compliance
Lightning Source LLC
Chambersburg PA
CBHW072041110526
44592CB00012B/1503